THE SHOTGUN BEHIND THE DOOR

Due Return Date Date	Due Return Date Date

THE
SHOTGUN
BEHIND
THE
DOOR

*Liberalism and the Problem of
Political Obligation*

PHILIP ABBOTT

THE
UNIVERSITY
OF GEORGIA
PRESS
ATHENS

Library of Congress Catalog Card Number: 74–84590
International Standard Book Number: 0–8203–0359–3

The University of Georgia Press, Athens 30602

Printed in the United States of America

FOR MY CHILDREN, JOSH AND MEG

Contents

Foreword

IN A CLIMATE of opinion still pervaded by liberal
political doctrine, why does the average sensual man feel
any obligation toward the political community? What sort
of bond is fancied self-interest? If, in vulgarized form,
the tenets of liberalism dominate most minds, who will
adventure much in defense of the common good? Will
not the ideologue with a shotgun, or perhaps the common
human predator with a shotgun, inherit the earth, as
liberal dogmas become insufficient to sustain a moral
order?

Such questions are raised perceptively by Philip Abbott
in this slim book. One thinks of a passage from George
Bernard Shaw's preface to *Back to Methuselah*:

> Goodnatured unambitious men are cowards when they have
> no religion. They are dominated and exploited not only by greedy
> and often halfwitted and half-alive weaklings who will do any-
> thing for cigars, champagne, motor cars, and the more childish
> and selfish uses of money, but by able and sound administrators
> who can do nothing else with them than dominate and exploit
> them. Government and exploitation become synonymous under
> such circumstances; and the world is finally ruled by the childish,
> the brigands, and the blackguards. Those who refuse to stand
> in with them are persecuted and occasionally executed when
> they give any trouble to the exploiters.

Just so. Mr. Abbott does not touch directly upon
religion as a source of political obligation, but he does
describe the decay of ethical obligation to the political
community, and shows how that decay is bound up with

liberal political theories. Can such a society stand against blackguards with shotguns? Mr. Abbott asks the right questions and suggests, at least, renewing approaches to this tremendous problem.

His is a closely reasoned study, succinct and interesting. Mr. Abbott has read intensively and widely, and so writes with authority. He has a power of analysis comparable to David Hume's, and is emancipated from ideological sentimentality. His distinctly is a philosophical cast of mind, and in part this book is a genuinely original contribution to its field — as well as a valuable examination of the failure of other writers, some of them distinguished scholars, to deal adequately with the difficulties of political obligation.

Mr. Abbott is especially acute in his dissection of liberals' insufficiency with respect to the concepts and realities of conscience and consent. His chapter on gratitude as sanction for obligation does not wholly dispose of gratitude – of what Gabriel Marcel calls "diffused gratitude" – as a possible satisfactory bond of society; yet Mr. Abbott's purpose here is to point out that the "odd debt of gratitude" is merely tacked on to liberalism. Therefore it cannot do duty, with the liberals, for a sound principle of obligation – whatever may be said of gratitude as sufficient in some nonliberal society.

His chapter on trust as a bond to secure (or improve) habitual obedience to political authority is seminal and exploratory; it deserves development at greater length. Several other portions of this book will wake minds.

The author deliberately restricts himself to *liberalism* in relation to political obligation. He mentions Marxism and democracy as adversaries of liberalism; he does not take up in detail the older doctrines of political obligation which are connected with what Leo Strauss calls the Great Tradition. Were he to do so, he would have to go all the way back to Solon, or earlier. He does touch with much understanding upon Plato, Hobbes, Hume, and Burke, recognizing in their writings certain devastating criticisms of current liberal orthodoxy on the question of political obligation.

It is quite conceivable that our society, or modern society generally, may be groping its way back toward such nonliberal understandings — in consequence, partially, of the altered and altering circumstances of mankind. Much may be rediscovered in Augustine, Aquinas, Richard Hooker, Montesquieu, Burke, and others. As Dicey, Santayana, and other writers have argued, liberalism may be only an evanescent phase, a product of nineteenth-century circumstances, now evaporating. As Mr. Abbott suggests late in this book, the liberal might find it well, logically, to strike "political obligation" from his vocabulary; but if that occurs, the liberal society may dissolve altogether, for want of moral convictions, without which no order endures.

Mr. James McAuley, in his book *The End of Modernity,* replies to certain remarks by Mr. Lionel Trilling on the failure of the liberal imagination. "If liberalist democracy is to be identified with liberalist negations and illusions, then every vital intellect will be bound to reject it with contempt," Mr. McAuley remarks. "But this is nonsense. Free institutions and representative government do not require the collapse of the mind into positivism or pragmatism or agnosticism; indeed, they will not indefinitely survive such a collapse."

Recognizing that indeed fallacious theory may betray us to the ruin of institutions, Mr. Abbott endeavors in this book to find a firmer footing for political obligation. No firm ground exists in the teachings of John Locke on consent and compact, he is acutely aware. In the citizens' trust, rather than in abstract notions of an unhistorical compact to which an imaginary people consented, Mr. Abbott finds hope of renewal.

Mr. Abbott ably relates theory to controversies of our day, and he offers us some lively hypothetical examples of the problems that arise in such concerns. He is free from cant. If this book is much read, and read especially by people who think of themselves as liberals, something will be accomplished toward the restoration of community and of political philosophy.

RUSSEL KIRK

Preface

IN SOME WAYS this is an ambitious work. I have attempted to resolve a major problem in one approach to political philosophy. But in an important sense *The Shotgun behind the Door* is a work in the style of what Locke described as the "underlaborer." It rests upon the visions, trials, and temptations of four centuries of liberal political philosophers.

Some time ago liberalism lost her title as the queen mother of modernity. Now she is regarded at best as more of a midwife. Other political philosophies appear to be more suited to deal with the problems of the day. American academicians have recently discovered this position, and their attack on the verities of liberalism in the past ten years has been voracious. Yet I have never been persuaded that the faults of liberalism can be traced to an inadequate conception of human nature nor that its political solutions represent institutionalized class greed. To the contrary, it has seemed to me that taken alone, the liberal's image of humanity and the political wisdom that has often been a result were on the whole sound and — dare I say it — even exhilarating truths. But somehow they have always been smashed or smothered by the efforts of liberals themselves.

Somehow liberals have never been able to present a successful accommodation between their ethical theories and the requirements of political order. To the extent to which actual governments have mirrored this failure, liberalism has not been entirely unfairly faulted for producing societies with severe injustices. The source of this problem can be found in the liberal's account of political obligation, which invariably assumes a baroque quality when compared to the possibilities offered in his larger theory.

The solution offered in these pages is unlikely to please many readers sympathetic to liberalism and still fewer who have already rejected it. It may not possess the features necessary to hold a society intact. Moreover, it may well be that one must reach back to periods before liberalism to derive a fuller account of political obligation. But that requires a more complex reformulation than can be offered in the preface and in fact is the focus of my current work.

Something less glorious than a resurrection of liberalism is the purpose of this book. I do believe that a polity of judicious citizens best reflects an appreciation of the danger of political power and the possibilities for individual development and that both of these are most clearly derived from the genius of liberalism. From my point of view the liberal legacy is one that we should not hastily reject.

I have incurred a great many debts for such a slim volume. The Ford Foundation awarded me a research fellowship for the 1972-73 year and the Earhart Foundation generously provided a summer grant. I have received thoughtful and constructive readings of various chapters from persons too numerous to mention. The final manuscript was read by René Williamson, Russel Kirk, Gordon S. Schochet, and Michael P. Riccards. I benefited greatly from their comments. Naturally responsibility for the views presented in these pages rests with the author. Kenneth Cherry and his staff at the University of Georgia

Press have provided me with invaluable support and guidance. My debt to my family is the largest. My wife, Patricia, encouraged me to pursue the complexities of political philosophy and introduced me to the rigor of the moral point of view both in philosophy and in daily life. This book is a small payment to my children for the joy they so freely give. It is dedicated to them with the sentiments expressed by John Adams who studied politics so that his children would "have the liberty to study mathematics and philosophy," in order to give their children "a right to study painting, poetry, music, architecture, statuary, tapestry and porcelain."

1

Political Obligation and the Liberal Imagination

I have sworn upon the altar of God, eternal hostility against every form of tyranny over the mind of man.

— Thomas Jefferson

IT IS AN IRONY of some significance that a tradition of political thought whose preoccupation with political obligation has made the problem the central task of modern political philosophy has failed to offer a satisfactory answer on its very own terms. The liberal must look with envy to the Marxist and the anarchist who simply deny the possibility of obligation to governments or to the democrat who uses the simplest arithmetic to reach his answers. For despite centuries of discussion on the nature and limits of the duties of a man to his state, the liberal tradition still faces the Marxist as well as the democrat unarmed, without a framework to defend himself. This essay, at least in part, is an attempt to reformulate the liberal response to the problem of political obligation by accepting the initial premises of liberal ethical theory and the political impulses that emerge from it while discarding the theories of political obligation that have been attached to it.

It has been the genius of liberalism to combine two contrary propositions about man and society. On the one hand the liberal has insisted upon the potentialities of human endeavor. Untrammeled by tradition, religion, and political despotism, the human spirit is capable of boundless creativity. In a sense Eric Voegelin is correct in tracing liberalism to the heresy of immanentism, the belief in the possibility of salvation on earth.

Benedict Spinoza, one not given to exult casually in human nature, spoke of the liberal ideal this way:

Man conceives a human character much more stable than his own, and sees that there is no reason why he should not himself acquire such a character. Thus he is led to seek means which will bring him to this pitch of perfection, and calls everything which will serve as such means a true good. The chief good is that he should arrive, together with other individuals, if possible, at the possession of the aforesaid character.[1]

In the *Spheres and Duties of Government* Wilhelm von Humboldt set forth his convictions by announcing that "the grand, leading principle, towards which every argument unfolded in these pages directly converges, is the absolute and essential importance of human development in its richest diversity."[2] For Thomas Jefferson the liberal ideal takes the form of an oath: "I have sworn upon the altar of God, eternal hostility against every form of tyranny over the mind of man."[3] What is so intriguing about his position is not so much the portrayal of the grandeur of the human spirit but the insistence that human development is to occur largely unaided by external structures. The liberal vision may be mighty but it is a very lonely one as well, without the benefit of the class solidarity of the Marxist or the communitarian fraternity of the democrat. This insistence upon the individuality of the pursuit of happiness has made liberalism acutely conscious of the importance of ethics and yet for the same reasons has provided it very serious difficulties in the formation of a political theory to take account of ethics.

Exacerbating this condition and alongside this faith lies the liberal belief in the corruptibility of the human spirit. Despite John Locke's belief that all men are rational and that the law of nature is set forth more clearly than positive laws, there are disagreements among "the most rational of men," and men are "in the dark" about the right thing to do. Jeremy Bentham gave this advice on his deathbed: "The way to be comfortable is to make others comfortable. The way to make others comfortable is to appear to love them. The way to appear to love them is to love them in reality." Nevertheless, he lays down a dictum called the first preference principle which every man ignores at his own peril: "Every human being is determined in every action by his judgment of what will produce the greatest happiness to himself, whatsoever the effect . . . in relation to the happiness of other similar beings, any or all of them taken together."[4]

Adam Smith spoke of fear and anxiety as the "great tormentors of the human breast."[5] For J. S. Mill the vision was even more horrific: "Nature impales men, breaks them as if on the wheel."[6] David Hume remarked on the frailty, the perverseness of our nature and despaired of the possibility of keeping men "faithfully and unerringly in the paths of justice."[7] For some liberal theorists this dimension of the human spirit involved the recognition of evil in the world; for others it was folly; for yet others it represented sloth and jealousy; and there were some for whom it was simply taken as a given, as the nature of the human condition.

There are two fundamental corollaries that have
become part of the liberal description of the human
condition. Taken together they form the liberal approach
to political obligation. The first is the belief that the
alternative conflict between reaching the heights of
human development and sinking to the depths of
human degradation, is unalterably a Manichean one.
Even Thomas Hobbes, most ambitious in regard to the
political resolution of the human condition, soberly
confessed that although the Leviathan could indeed
be made immortal, even he could not devise a system
which could channel human passion permanently. The
directions that societies as well as individuals may take,
then, is always reversible. In a Golden Age of peace,
security, and human development, Adam Smith warned
that men were "at all times surrounded by unknown
ememies."[8] Hobbes chided his readers, anticipating their
disbelief at his propositions regarding human nature,
by asking why, in a well-settled state with the majesty
of the law to overawe wrongdoers, do we still lock our
doors at night? But when affairs run poorly, the liberal
is led to reject the claim that misery is a permanent condition. John Adams's concern with connection between
revolution and terror was answered by Jefferson in this
fashion:

The generation which commences a revolution rarely completes
it. Habituated from their infancy to passive submission of body
and mind to their kings and priests, they are not qualified when
called on to think and provide for themselves, and their inex-
perience, their ignorance and bigotry make them instruments
often, in the hands of the Bonapartes and Iturbides, to defeat
their own rights and purposes. This is the present situation of
Europe and Spanish America. . . . A first attempt to recover
the right of self-government may fail, so may a second, a third,
etc. But as a younger and more instructed race comes on, the

sentiment becomes more and more intuitive and a fourth, a fifth of some subsequent one of the ever renewed attempts will ultimately succeed. . . . To attain all this, however, rivers of blood must yet flow and years of desolation pass over.[9]

Locke refused to accept that men were "a Herd of Inferior Creatures" as Mill denied the belief that men must always remain children politically. Immanuel Kant even claimed that the asocial human qualities were essential to human progress. It has been especially difficult for the contemporary liberal to justify belief in humanity in a century which has seen technology reduce evil to bureaucratic formality. But even in the squalor and shamelessness of a concentration camp, some have reported soberly of the quality of humanity. Bruno Bettelheim reports of an inmate about to be led to the gas chamber. A Nazi officer, having learned that the woman was once a dancer, orders her to perform. She does and for a finale grabs the officer's gun, shoots him and other guards. She was, of course, executed on the spot. Bettelheim claims:

But isn't it probable that despite the grotesque setting in which she danced, dancing made her once again a person? Dancing, she was singled out as an individual, asked to perform in what had once been her chosen vocation. . . . Despite the hundreds of thousands of living dead men who moved quietly to their graves, this one example, and there were several like her, shows that in an instant the old personality can be regained, its destruction undone, once we decide on our own that we wish to cease being units in a system.[10]

The second corollary, one which is certain to be disputed, is the inability of liberalism to fix itself permanently on the source of human frailty. The liberal has never enjoyed the certitude that the Marxist shares in his commitment to the proletariat if perhaps only because his origin in the middle classes has led to alternating enmity and support from the outer crusts of society. But more to the point, the liberal preoccupation with individual autonomy and development in the context of the extreme fragility of a moral existence has prevented liberalism from becoming the class ideology that its detractors have claimed it to be. Wereas in different periods, liberals have found moral autonomy best exemplified in the country squire or entrepreneur and have identified its villains with kings or judges or majorities, liberalism's own ethical theory has often become an argument against firm class embodiment of its ideal. Locke may have attempted to alter his definition of individual autonomy to exclude the practice of slavery in America but the devices available to him were so limited that they can be separated from his doctrine of natural rights without even so much as marring the internal consistency of the original theory. James Madison sees property as the chief cause of civil strife, and while he believes that its ownership reflects intelligence and industry, nevertheless their qualities do not exclude the landed gentry from those men who are not angels. Mill moved from a laissez-faire economics to protest the "torment" of industrialization. Jefferson agonized between the implications of his political theory and his own inclinations in regard to slavery.

Yet if its ethical theory has not permitted liberalism to move as gracefully from ethics to sociology as Marxism is able to do, neither has it been able to wed its ethical theory to an account of politics. For government, as Thomas Paine said, is like man's dress, a badge of lost innocence. The palaces of kings are built upon the ruins of the bowers of paradise, for alas, "the impulses of conscience are not clear, uniform or irresistibly obeyed."[11] For Paine the origins of politics lie in wickedness. For Kant, the problem involved finding political order for a "race of devils." Bentham advised his readers to see every man in power as a possible thief. Locke's civil society arose from "Passion," "Revenge," "Interest," "Corruption," "Partiality." And there is a very basic consistency in the liberal position on this point. For once the autonomy of men has been asserted and asserted so eloquently, the recommendation of political order becomes the supreme sacrifice to the liberal vision. Bentham wrote that the "whole of government" was a connected series of sacrifices. This position becomes even more tragic when one reflects for a moment upon the historical circumstances of the early liberals. The government represented the gaol, the royal courts the tower, and its writs the practice of "quartering." The dilemma of liberalism, then, has been to formulate a theory of duties to an institution which by its nature is evil: in principle, since it restricts the exercise of individual moral judgment, and in practice, in that it shows an almost magnetic attraction toward corruption.

There is a popular lyric that notes the difficulty of talking to a man with a shotgun in his hand. It is precisely this image of the state that has created liberalism and has since haunted the liberal mind. It is extremely difficult to envisage a man reaching an independent moral judgment, especially assuming the liberal doubts about seeing clearly one's duty, and acting freely upon it when faced with such imminent distraction. Suppose we even assume that the man with the shotgun is asking us for some laudable sacrifice. Someone approaches you with a shotgun aimed at your face or just resting languidly on his waist and asks you to contribute some money ("anything you can afford") to the American Cancer Society. The distinction between request and demand immediately dissolves as your eyes fix upon the barrel of the gun. Your decision does not revolve around sorting out your until now unfocused duties. After all, moral philosophers excepted, we rarely order our moral priorities until situations call upon us to do so. Should your money be spent on new shoes for your son, saved for some future event, or given to this immediate need? Your decision is now focused upon the "request" and your own security. The calculation now rests upon considerations of morality and prudence. And given the difficulty involved in distinguishing between the course of morality and prudence in the best of circumstances, your motives, once you decide to offer a "contribution," are hopelessly muddled. The liberal has now for three hundred years been devising ways to construct a door between the man with the gun and the citizen but every liberal is aware that the situation is not qualitatively altered if we do not actually see the gun. (How different might our politics be if the president, congressmen, and judges would walk about, as revolutionaries often do, with pistols on their hips!) Nor is it altered if we elect the man who is to carry it, or if we require, in fail-safe fashion, two or three men to discharge its blast.

The image we have constructed is one of near hopelessness but only because of the liberal vision discussed above. It is not the purpose of this essay to demean the efforts of those men who have devised constitutions and suggested innumerable social and economic practices to keep the shotgun behind the door. It is rather to suggest that the liberal has sacrificed the genius of his ethical theory to the political wisdom which emerges from it. Plagued by the image of the shotgun behind the door, the liberal has justified government by the only appeal available to him, prudence. But rather than keep his ethical and political theories separate and intact, he has sacrificed his moral theories by linking them to the requirements of political order or serving them upon the altar of interest. This has ultimately led to a denial of the problem of political obligation itself, the raison d'etre of the liberal vision.

The history of the liberal approach to political obligation is a history of frustrations, a network of alternatives taken and rejected resembling the maze which confronted Lewis Carroll's Alice. The search for a solution has reflected, of course, the variations which liberalism has undergone itself. Yet beneath the complexity of liberalism and the contortions which its ethical theories have undergone to meet the challenge of political obligation rests a basic framework within which liberals have been forced to labor. For the liberal, political action is to be limited to what contemporary economists and political scientists call "collective goods," benefits which can only accrue to the citizenry as a body. The problem with this view of political action is that it requires additional propositions in order to formulate a design for political order. Since from the viewpoint of the individual, it is still possible to obtain the benefits from the existence of collective goods without contributing to them, the liberal is placed in the position of justifying compulsory "payments" to the community through political organization. And since the liberal vision emphasizes that the procedural or determinative aspect of morality is crucial to the existence of ethics, external compulsion requires other than a moral justification through political organization. Reliance upon traditional forms of compliance other than force, such as tradition or religion, are violations of the liberal concept of morality as well. In short, the liberal is without a conceptual vocabulary to justify the state. The road to finding one's moral duty is very narrow, however; and since it is the liberal belief that even should all individuals manage to remain on it, there is no assurance of harmony, political organization is in need of some justification. The liberal has attempted to meet this problem in three basic ways.

The contract

The idea of a social contract binding both ruler and ruled to certain principles of political organization is perhaps the most shopworn of all liberal political theories. It has become a theory employed with best results by those in political power. Yet the contract model of political obligation was once a revolutionary doctrine because it indicated that those who govern are to be held accountable in some fashion to those who are governed. We will expend some effort in chapter 3 to show the basic futility in this belief but our task now is to indicate the popularity of the contract model among liberal theorists. We will confine our comments here to an analysis of John Locke because a treatment of other consent theorists follows and because Locke's position, despite its overall plodding whigishness, provides us with an important thrust to a revised account of political obligation.

Locke begins his *Second Treatise* with what is

historically a startling position. Men "by Nature, are free, equal and independent," "the Natural Liberty of Man is to be free from any Superior Power on Earth, and not under the will or Legislative Authority of Man."[12] Yet the state of nature is not a state of license — no one ought to "take away, or impair the life, or what tends to Life, Liberty, Health, Limbs or Goods of another."[13] If we assume that Locke's state of nature is a description of a condition in which men are free to accept or reject the moral point of view without the intercession of any social or political authority, we have a fair description of the liberal view of the human condition. Equality in the state of nature is moral: "All the Power and Jurisdiction is reciprocal, no one having more than another. . . . This equality of Men by Nature, the Judicious Hooker looks upon as so evident in itself, and beyond all question, that he makes it the Foundation of that obligation to mutual Love amongst Men on which he Builds the Duties they owe one another."[14] Hobbes makes the equality of men in the state of nature an equality of power or force. While there is this sort of equality in Locke's model, when it comes into consideration a new environment is constructed, one in which reciprocity is abandoned. One need no longer treat the transgressor as another with the same rights and duties as himself but as a "Brute," a "Beast of Prey." While the state of nature may melt dangerously into a state of war, Locke keeps both concepts analytically separately identifiable and, it would appear, at least empirically possible.

The solution to the social "inconveniences" of moral autonomy is known to every American schoolboy. Men agree to "unite into one Political Society" and it is this agreement which defines the basis of the entire political system:

> Nor can any Edict of any Body else, in what Form soever conceived, or by what Power soever backed have the force and obligation of a Law which has not its sanction from that Legislature, which the public has chosen and appointed. For without this the law could not have that, which is absolutely necessary to its being a law, the consent of Society . . . and therefore all the obedience, which by the most solemn ties any one can be obliged to pay, alternately terminates in this Supreme Power.[15]

Locke's troubles begin almost immediately when he attempts to determine the significance of the contract as an avenue to moral duty. One who consents is *"perpetually* and *indispensably* obliged to be and remain *unalterably* a subject to it else it would be like Cato's entering a theatre, signifying nothing." (emphasis mine) [16] The oath is regarded with such importance that it cannot be considered given by inheritance (One "cannot by any Compact whatsoever, bind his children or Posterity") or habit ("People take no notice of it, and thinking it not done at all or not necessary conclude they are naturally subjects as they are men") .[17] Yet the remainder of the *Second Treatise* is a series of devices designed alternately to restrict and enlarge the moral debts incurred by the contract. And most important for our purposes, the contract is left unnoticed like some errant relative during the raison d'être of the *Second Treatise,* the justification of revolution. Unlike the format of the Declaration of Independence, the *Second Treatise* does not offer a list of promises broken. Its focus is upon the arbitrary and destructive nature of state power as a violation of natural law: the government has "impoverished," "harassed," "enslaved," "subdued" the people by "Arbitrary and Irregular Commands."[18]

Privatization of moral judgment

One way in which the liberal can connect his ethical theories with political organization is to privatize the liberal moral vision itself. By emphasizing the considerable nonmoral influences upon individual moral judgment, the liberal is able to keep pure his commitment to individual autonomy but views its implementation in terms so fragile as to make it unnecessary to account for in his political philosophy. It was Hobbes, of course, who was most successful with this approach, and many liberals who have employed this method have worked only to remove the sharpness from Hobbes's position. For Hobbes begins his *Leviathan* with an account of human autonomy more rigid than outlined by any other theorists. Men are by nature equal, none are so weak or dull witted to allow us to speak of qualitative differences. The Hobbesian man asserts his autonomy brazenly; he is not restrained by religion or habit or even what the eighteenth-century philosophers were to call moral sentiment. Yet, naturally enough the results involve "horrible calamities," the life of man is "nasty, solitary, brutish and short." Hobbes achieves his desired effect by radically privatizing the moral dimension. The concept of conscience is nothing more than each man's judgment riddled with the passions and shortsighted interests that so characterize the reasoning of the Hobbesian man. Only by making the objects of men's desires public, that is, observable to other men, is Hobbes able to construct the logical masterpiece of the *Leviathan* and nearly succeed in actually constructing a system of ethics from prudence. Yet even in Hobbes's gloomy world a flicker of the liberal vision emerges, although it is almost an obscene product of the logic of the *Leviathan.* The subject, although he has authorized the sovereign to sentence him to death should reason of state demand it, still has the right of resistance. Why else, Hobbes asks, does the state bind the hands of the man about to be hanged?

But the radical privatization of the moral judgment can result in other political positions equally as damaging to the liberal vision. If we exchange but a few propositions, the *Leviathan,* which at least has the advantage of a clarity of expression, dissolves into the murky despotism of the conservative state. Hume's analyses, which have presented as severe a challenge to modern liberals as Hobbes's, are a case in point.

Hume contended that of the two ways in which men can perceive reality, ideas and impressions, it is the latter that largely provide the medium through which the world is known. Since impressions are irrational or, more accurately, prerational, the significance of reason is further limited. Not only is it impossible to reason from innate ideas of the mind, but it is also unlikely that reason plays much of a role in the experiential setting. It was Hume's firm belief that the mind resting in an experiential prison cannot establish the necessity of any action since it is a tool limited on the one hand by the objects that are fed into it and on the other hand by the passions of man's nature that required a departure from Hobbes's resolution of political conflict. For Hume found it necessary to write moral and political philosophy without the "key" that Hobbes offers his readers for use in his introduction to *Leviathan.*

Although Hume had put the assumptions of natural law, even the Hobbesian version, to disrepute through his own analysis of human knowledge, it still remained for him to account for the fact that men indeed operated in a context that seemed to point to the existence of a rational metaphysics. They speak about justice, good and evil, about virtues and vice; they approve of some actions, disapprove of others. It is Hume's phychological theory that explains away this phenomena and begins to provide for the construction of what he regarded as a descriptive theory of society. For Hume, man has two parts to his nature: affections and understandings. Since the latter is essentially a passive attribute which Hume has made void of political significance, we will concern ourselves first with the affections. Man operates according to natural and artificial motives. He is capable of seeing another in pain and feeling a sense of sympathy for the victim. The motivation is spontaneous and not based upon reflection, although Hume speculates that the beholder's reactions may in part be based upon the fact that he was once in a similar position or that he can imagine such a position. In any case, the motivation of the sympathizer is not self-interest, and when a third party views the reaction with approval it is not self-regarding. Generally, however, men by "nature" act according to their "self-love" regardless of the opinions of their peers. On the other hand, a man can be made to act according to "artificial" virtue which can accommodate his own self-interest or can be unrelated to it. This self-interest may be immediate or long-range. But his decision here is reached by reflection on the consequences of his action. Or, in the case of a long-range consequence, it may be influenced by his social environment acting on him through education or taught by precept. His action is held in esteem by others either because it is in their interest to view it so or because they have been accustomed to react so. From these categories we can see that an action, be it prompted by natural or artificial reasons, is virtuous or moral only in reference to their approval or disapproval, not in reference to the action itself or to its motivation. And when such actions are considered by others as moral or virtuous, they assume the qualities of duties, the significance of which we will soon discuss.

Men, then, have a variety of options open to them. According to Hume, human nature will generally take the course demanded by self-love in the absence of external restraints. What then produces these external restraints, and in what sense, if any, can human nature be ameliorated under these new conditions? Hume gives us the "first and original principle of human society": "This necessity is no other than that natural appetite betwixt the sexes, which unites them together, and preserves their union, till a new tye takes place in their concern for their common offspring."[19] But the rise of the familial unit does not ameliorate but increases the defects of human nature. The extent of benevolence may broaden quantitatively but the principle of "self-love" does not increase qualitatively — the relationships between families are still governed by our "natural temper": "For while each person loves himself better than any other single person, and his love to others bears the greatest affection, this must necessarily produce an opposition of passions and a consequent opposition of actions, which cannot but be dangerous to the new-established union".[20] The remedy to this "inconvenience" cannot be found in "any inartificial principle of the human mind." The idea of justice "would never have been dreamed of among rude and savage men." Here Hume's argument proceeds consistently with his epistemology: "This partiality, then, and unequal affection, must not only have an influence on our behavior and conduct in society, but even on our ideas of vice and virtue; so as to make us regard any remarkable trangression of such a degree of partiality, either by too great an enlargement, or contraction of the affections, as vicious and immoral."[21] Thus a person operating under a principle of universal affections would be condemned as immoral and unjust. When, then, and how does society become established and a concept of justice arise? Hume answers that both arrive together. Man's "qualities of mind," selfishness and confined generosity, along with the situation of external objects, the scanty provision nature has made for his wants, make society the only vehicle "able to supply his defects" and provide the origin of justice. Had man been endowed with universal generosity and perfect abundance of material, the very idea of justice would be destroyed simply because it would be useless. Hume now asserts explicitly that the origin of justice is not only a device to regulate the self-interest of man and that a sense of justice "is not founded on our ideas, but on our impressions," and those impressions "are not natural to the mind of man but arise from artifice and human conventions."[22]

But Hume's separation of the obligation to obey promises and the obligation to obey government allows him to complete his theory. Heretofore Hume had confined his attention to the amelioration of human nature through the growth of society. The "small uncultivated society" can be maintained without the institution of government. But as society grows larger, interests become more remote and fail to contain the pursuit of immediate interests. So when some men in a more complex society "perceive the necessity of government to maintain peace and execute justice," government, *upon its first establishment,* would naturally be supposed to derive its obligation from those laws of nature and, in particular, from that concerning the performance of promises.[23] Since a promise is already in existence attended with a moral obligation, it is the original sanction of government, the source of the first obligation to obedience. Hume, however, criticizes this conclusion as it becomes the foundation of "our fashionable system of politics." Hume's position is that obedience may initially be grafted to the obligation of promises but that it soon takes root of itself and has an original obligation and authority, independent of all contracts. The argument against seeing government as an institution, which is based upon the promises of two parties, governors and governed, is rejected by Hume on three grounds. The first is based upon his psychological theory and proceeds on two points. It concerns the relationship between civil duty and natural laws. The former is invented for the sake of the latter. "The principal object of government is to contain men to observe the laws of nature."[24] Its exact observance is the effect of the institution of government and is not the obedience to government as an effect of the obligation of a promise. Furthermore, the interest in obeying government and the interest in obeying promises are separate interests and require separate obligations: "To obey the civil magistrate is requisite to preserve order and concord in society. To perform promises is requisite to beget mutual trust and confidence in the common offices of life. The ends, as well as the means, are perfectly distinct, nor is the one subordinate to the other."[25]

This argument is buttressed by empirical observations of political activity and of anthropological speculation. While Hume's arguments about the historical plausibility of a social contract are often passed off as unnecessary to the viability of the contract model, they are pertinent in terms of his own conception of ethics and pertinent to those who share his position on the nature of morality. The origin of government probably arose from the exigencies of wars. "Their frequency gradually produced an habitual and, if you please to call it so, a voluntary, and therefore precarious, acquiescence in the people."[26] The principle of obeying promises is much too sophisticated for savages.[27] Furthermore, the principle of contract is today unknown to much of the world. Princes claim subjects as their property and assert their independent right of sovereignty from conquest or succession. Absolute governments punish subjects freely for what they call treason and rebellion. Hume's "clear proof" of the fact that obedience rests elsewhere than consent epitomizes the nature of his approach: "But as that [arbitrary government] is as natural and common a government as any, it certainly occasions some obligation; and is plain from experience that men, who are subject to it, do always think so."[28]

Consent as a basis of political obligation is rejected because it runs contrary to Hume's observations on human experience. What then are the reasons for which men obey government? The general answer to this question is provided negatively by Hume's philosophical position. Men do not obey government because they are bound by the laws of natural justice or natural law to do so. Justice has already been dispensed with as an invention of man designed to cope with his needs and resources. "Obedience is a new duty which must be invented to support that of justice."[29] Obedience, then, is as artificial as justice since both concepts are based upon their utility to man. Reason also plays but a little part in the political obedience because man will more often than not follow his immediate interests which are dictated by his passions rather than obey his remote interests which dictate that it is advantageous for him to obey authority. In fact, it is the task of government to "oblige men, however reluctant, to consult their real and permanent interest."[30] This is accomplished by making it the immediate interest of the governors to make the governed aware of their real yet distant advantages in obedience. The genesis of political obedience for Hume is utility. The public interest lies "in the sense of the general advantage which is reaped from government." This utility, however, assumes moral rather than rational proportions. Public morality arises from the exigencies of the relationships between human nature and the scarcity of goods in the external environment; in short, utility is the midwife of morality. But the moral character of obligation rests not in its utility but in how men feel about them. Breach of contract or rebellion are vices not because they contradict the long-range interests of man, but because they are viewed with disapproval by peers. Other men's approval or disapproval of actions in civil society convert rules of convenience into rules of right. Thus, for Hume, artificial moral rules are the basis of obedience to the state. Artificial morality is reinforced by habit. "Habit soon consolidates what other principles of human nature had imperfectly found; and men, once accustomed to obedience, never think of departing from that path."[31]

As for other bases of obedience that have received considerable attention from other writers, Hume contends that they suppose the antecedent influence of opinions or artificial morality. Men obey out of fear only when they are tempted to disobey.[32] Affection as a strong basis of obligation has been rejected in Hume's psychological theories. Self-interest or the expectation of particular rewards does not suffice to cover all the population.

What in Hume's political theory are the limits and extent of this obedience? An appeal to resistance on natural principles based upon reason or God has been eliminated. The breach of original contract has been divorced from the right to disobey. That the government operates contrary to or in the absence of the consent of the governed is no limit to obedience since this principle is neither universal nor necessary to the "natural" laws of society. In fact, all these invocations are only grounds for a particular duty to obey — not grounds for a general duty to obey. They do not determine the limits of our duty but the persons toward whom we have the duty. And although Hume lists several principles to judge who deserves obedience, he concludes that it is usually best to accept whatever principle confirms the authority of those who actually govern.

Are there then no limits to the obedience of the governed in Hume's theory? Hume does tell us that "anxious care and solicitude in stating all cases in which resistance may be allowed" is "preposterous."[33] If any education is to be done, it should be the inculcation of obedience. But this same philosopher does justify the removal of King James II for "mistaking the nature of our constitution." The limits to obedience, then, occur "when the public is in the highest danger from violence and tyranny." At this point civil obedience yields to "the primary and original obligation" — "*salus populi suprema lex."* In this context obedience is dependent upon a utilitarian theory of obligation. Government was created for its social utility; when that government ceases to supply that function, duty to it ends. But, if we recall, the primary basis of political obligation was not so much its utility, which is· perceived by few, but a moral — albeit artificial obligation. Since a characteristic of its moral content is the attitude of others toward it, political obligation ceases only when acts of rebellion are widespread and approved by the populace.

The privatization of morality does, of course, resolve the liberal dilemma of providing for a moral justification of political authority by eliminating any public vocabulary of ethics. In fact, as we shall see when we discuss ethical noncognitivism, the contemporary version of this alternative, it allows the liberal to dissolve the category of political obligation altogether. But the price is very dear since it eliminates the greatest contribution of liberalism to political theory, the moral evaluation of political authority itself. For if the privatization of moral judgment is so complete as to allow for the justification of the state by extreme prudence or habit, the citizen is also robbed of any communicable validity to moral objections to his government. In short, the liberal dilemma is resolved by forsaking liberalism itself.

Superiority of interest

We have noted that Hume, in his attempt at the destruction of the contract, substituted a utility-*cum*-habit model of political obligation. Adam Smith, in his *Theory of Moral Sentiments,* continued the assault on the social contract yet refused to accept Hume's conclusions. What emerges in Smith's *Moral Sentiments* is an ethical theory of much plausibility evolved only to be shattered against the perceived necessities of political order. Smith begins first by rejecting the concept of a moral sense as an explanation of ethics presented by his popular predecessor Francis Hutcheson. The idea of a separate moral faculty fails to explain the wide divergence of judgment on what is good and evil. Yet the standard of utility as the basis of ethics is criticized as well. Usefulness is not the original justification of approbation or approval. They may enhance our moral sentiments but they are not a justifiable explanation of them. Hume is criticized for making the moral point of view equivalent to the standard used to judge a "convenient or well-contrived building." There are other reasons for "praising a man than that for which we praise a chest of drawers."[34]

In substitution for both moral sense and utility, Smith offers the idea of an internal monitor — the "man" or "demigod" "within the breast." This impartial spectator within us determines the worthiness of our conduct by placing ourselves in the position of others and momentarily, at least, appreciating another's needs or distress. Smith describes his version of moral judgments this way:

As to the eye of the body, objects appear great or small, not so much according to their real dimensions as according to the nearness or distance of their situation, so do they likewise to what may be called the natural eye of the mind; and we remedy the defects of both these organs pretty much in the same matter. In my present situation, an immense landscape of lawns and woods and distant mountains seems to do no more than cover the little window which I write by, and to be out of all proportion less than the chamber in which I am sitting. I can form a just

comparison between those great objects and the objects around
us in no other way than by transporting myself, at least in fancy,
to a different station, from whence I can survey both at nearly
equal distances and thereby form some judgment of their proportions. . . . In the same manner, to the selfish and original
passions of human nature, the loss or gain of a very small interest
of our own appears to be of vastly more importance, excites
a much more passionate joy or sorrow, a much more ardent
desire or aversion, than the greatest concern of another with
whom we have no particular connexion. His interests, as long
as they are surveyed from his station, can never be put into
balance with our own, can never restrain us from doing whatever
may tend to promote our own, however ruinous to him. Before
we can make any proper comparison of those opposite interests,
we must change our position. We must view them neither from
our own place nor yet from his, neither with our own eyes nor
yet with his, but from the place and with the eyes of a third
person who has no particular connexion with either, and who
judges with impartiality between us.[35]

For Smith "this is the only looking-class by which
we can in some measure, with the eyes of other people,
scrutinize the propriety of our own conduct." It is this
"great judge" of our conduct that allows Smith to escape
the privatization or habitualization of moral judgment
demanded by Hobbes and Hume respectively. But if
"the great inmate of the breast" has considerable
influence on our conduct he is not omnipotent. For there
is also a "man without" as well as a "man within."
While the latter desires praiseworthiness, the former
desires only praise itself. The impartial spectator may
receive information resulting in reports very different
from what circumstances authorize. The man within
may be a "vicegerent upon earth" but he is only the
court of first appeal — the all-seeing judge of the world
decides moral controversies authoritatively.[36] And, of
course, we receive his judgment in another life.

Smith applies the impartial spectator to the contract theory and arrives at an observation unmatched for its political acuteness and common sense:

It may indeed be said that by remaining in the country you tacitly consent to the contract and are bound to it. But how can you avoid staying in it? You were not consulted whether you should be born in it or not. And how can you get out of it? Most people know no other language nor country, are poor, and obliged to stay not far from the place where they were born to labour for a subsistence. They cannot, therefore, be said, to give any consent to a contract, though they have the strongest sense of obedience. To say that by staying in a country a man agrees to a contract of government is just the same with carrying a man into a ship and after he is at a distance from land to tell him that by being in the ship he has contracted to obey the master.[37]

But when Smith sets about to offer his own version of political obligation he blindfolds the eyes of the impartial spectator. We are told that there are two principles which induce men to enter in a civil society, authority and utility. Smith lists four attributes which give one man authority over another: superior age, superior abilities of body and of mind, ancient family, and superior wealth. Each attribute justifies authority in different societies. In a "warlike society he is a man of superior strength, and in a polished one, of superior mental capacity."[38] But since "superior abilities of body and mind are not so easily judged by others," it is more "convenient" to give the preference to riches.[39] As to the second principle, utility, everyone is sensible of the necessity of "this principle to preserve justice and peace in the society." We submit to civil authority to avoid even "greater evils."

Smith makes a brief attempt to connect his principle of authority to the reasoning of impartial spectator by noting that we have a strong propensity to pay respect to our superiors: "We admire their happy situation, enter into it with pleasure and endeavor to promote it."[40] But this is clearly the "man without" that Smith has speaking. He is not the man who stands apart as a third person who refuses to judge from his own eyes or with another's, but the one who joins in with the fortunes of his peers. The impartial spectator would submit to the judgments of the rich only when he has proven to himself the merits of individual effort and the economic system which allows it to flourish, not when he has savored by a very active imagination the comforts of wealth. Similarly the principle of utility, as described by Smith, appeals to the self-love that the impartial spectator is designed to counteract. Even when Smith considers resistance, he does so without the "great Judge's" aid: "It may sometimes be for my *interest* to disobey, and to wish government overturned, but I am sensible that other men are of a different opinion and would not assist me in the enterprise."[41]

If obedience to the state rests upon a principle no higher than interest, then, of course restrictions upon those in political authority have only the same limit. And we all know that they have a better chance of implementing their interests than the citizen has of his. Smith's advice is in an ironic sense appropriate: "No government is quite perfect, but it is better to submit to some inconveniences than make attempts against it."[42] Ultimately when his ethical theory is called upon to meet its most severe challenge, the moral evaluation of political authority, Smith has us judging the state for the reasons he had castigated Hume, by the standard we use in judging a "chest of drawers."

Yet Smith's account of political obligation is saved from such a harsh conclusion, at least internally, because of the very genteel nature of his utilitarianism and view of society in general. His works taken together show an almost unconscious belief in a preestablished harmony. It is only the more modest task of noting the principles which have contributed to its establishment which Smith set out for himself. If we take away the supervision of providence, if only for one awful moment, we see the grave difficulties which liberalism faces when it sets out to base its politics on interest. But that effort was to be undertaken by a much more brash and less pleasant personage, Jeremy Bentham.

Bentham's ethics correspond very much to Smith's, with the latter's veneer of civility and eloquence stripped away. For Bentham the doctrine of natural rights used to support social contract theory was "rhetorical non-sense — nonsense upon stilts." There is no mention, as Mill sadly notes, of words like "conscience" of "prin-ciple" or "moral duty" among Bentham's springs of action unless they can be regarded as synonyms for "love of reputation" or "religious motive". Bentham even outdoes Smith on the question of governmental regulation of interest rates. For Bentham the whole of ethics must be submitted to the principle of utility, "the greatest good for the greatest number," and moral judgment tied to a "felicific calculus." What is so crucial in Bentham's system, however, is his justification of the principle of utility itself. The *Principles of Morals and Legislation* begins with the admonition that tenets of other ethical systems dissolve either into the principle of utility or suffer under hopeless logical inconsistencies. But the challenge which Bentham offers is already rigged. For when he asks at the end of the first chapter "admitting (what is not true) that the word *right* can have a meaning without reference to utility, let him say whether there is any such thing as a motive that a man can have to pursue the dictates of it: if there is, let him say what that motive is, and how it is to be distinguished from those which enforce the dictates of utility: if not then lastly let him say what it is this other principle can be good for,"[43] he has already declared pain and pleasure the two sovereign masters under which nature has placed mankind. If men live in the pleasure-pain prison that he tells us they do, then of course it is impossible for any of us to operate from any motive other than utility. Since all human action is "interested," it is impossible to envision an action which in Bentham's words is not "self-regarding." No writer could have assured us of the likelihood of all men acting morally as confidently as Bentham could, since Bentham constructed a system in which action based upon self-interest was moral. The only link which allows Bentham to speak of happiness for the greatest number is the assumption that a society based upon that principle contributes to individual happiness as well.

Since government is the institution in society most clearly associated with pain and punishment, "it is itself one vast evil" and Bentham prefers to restrict its functions. "Men let them but once clearly understand one another, will not be long ere they agree."[44] Even the governmental regulation of interest rules were regarded by Bentham as evidence of "maternal care, the tacking of leading strings upon the backs of grown persons."[45] The problem of politics only lay in securing a lasting connection between the "self-preference" principle, every man's concern with his own happiness, and "the right and proper end of government," the greatest happiness of the greatest number.[46] For Bentham the failure of such a coincidence lay largely with officials of government. Through most of his life Bentham attacked those features of government which he felt impeded his "golden age" — constitution and ancestor worship, judges, monarchy, sinecures, restricted suffrage, the established church, and the House of Lords. The problem lay in devising practices which would lead the governors to pursue "universal interests" for the enjoyment of the greatest number rather than "sinister interests" for the enjoyment of the few. His solution was to minimize confidence in government and maximize responsibility. His constitutional code recommends not only universal suffrage, annual parliaments, and vote by ballot, but competitive examinations and bidding for lowest salaries for bureaucrats. He even suggests reduction in salary for legislative nonattendance, provided a verified infirmary treatment could not be produced.

Yet despite this vigorous distrust of political authority, the concept of sinister interests does not remain exclusive to the governors when Bentham discusses political obligation. He tells us that obedience to the state ought to involve calculations of the "probable mischiefs of obedience" as against "the probable mischiefs of resistance."[47] Insisting that one's duty to obey is synonymous with one's interest to obey ("it is their duty to obey, just so long as it is their interest, and no longer"),[48] Bentham loses his usual confidence in offering criteria. "It is improbable to find an answer" — one must, however, consider "his own internal persuasion of a balance of utility on the side of resistance."[49] When confronted with the core problem of duty to political authority, the "first preference principle" is very cautiously connected to the possibility of sinister interests, this time on the part of the citizenry.

The range of political authority "must unavoidably
. . . unless where limited by express convention, be
allowed to be indifinite."⁵⁰ And, of course, if the word
duty is an inappropriate word to define citizen's
relationship to government, it is, despite all of Bentham's tirades against official arrogance and corruption,
inappropriate to the governors as well: "The word 'duty'
if applied to persons spoken of as supreme governors,
is evidently applied to them in a sense which is
figurative and improper."⁵¹

Bentham's theory of ethics, intended as a broadaxe
against corruption and irresponsibility, was so sharpened
by his doctrine of self-interest that when it came time
to apply it to political obligation it left only a paper
cut, razor-thin and harmless. The first preference
principle had to be applied, sooner or later, to the
governed as well as the governors. When it came to
the problem of political obligation, the fear that social
harmony might not exist led Bentham to use his weapon
against those he had sought to free. Yet even in Bentham's lifetime those doubts about an automatic con-
vergence between individual and community interest
began to fully surface. In "Government", and "Education," James Mill confronted the problem and offered,
almost breathlessly, a solution. "Political education"
is the "keystone of the arch" of a just government.
Mill's conception of education was so wide (familial
and social — the influence of our neighbors as well
as "technical," formal schooling) that he contended
it could only be undertaken by the "political machinery
of government." If government would only undertake
the effort to show that "the natural prizes of just
and virtuous conduct" are the true objects of our
desire, "it is natural to see diffused among mankind a

generous ardor in the acquisition of those admirable qualities which prepare a man for admirable action, great intelligence, perfect self-command, and over-ruling benevolence."⁵² In Mill's opinion, these characteristics were already held by the middle class. The function of government would be to hold up this class as a model to the lower orders of society and "account it an honour" for its children to imitate them. Then, the laborers would certainly be fit for political power.

What providence and universal self-interest was unable to manage can now be attained through class tutelage. Even with James's son, John Stuart, whose self-doubts about utilitarianism brought liberalism to its first major crisis, "political education" remains the "keystone of the arch." Pushpin can only be preferred to poetry *after* one can say he is acquainted with both.

Modern liberalism has continued to follow in the footsteps of a truncated Benthamism. Its positions are quite complicated but it can, I think, be reduced to two propositions. The first is extracted from Mill's critique of Benthamite utilitarianism and was developed most forcefully by T. H. Green. It contends that the goal of morality is the development of the individual's personality:

The condition of a moral life is the possession of will and reason. Will is the capacity in a man of being determined to action by the idea of a possible satisfaction of himself. An act of will is an action so determined. A state of will is the capacity as determined by the particular objects in which the man seeks self-satisfaction; and it becomes a character in so far as the self-satisfaction is habitually sought in objects of a particular kind. Practical reason is the capacity in a man of conceiving the perfection of his nature as an object to be attained by action. All moral ideas have their origin in reason (i.e., in the idea of a possible self-perfection to be attained by the moral agent.)⁵³

The second proposition assigns the state the task of aiding this individual self-perfection. This is the justification of the state and this is the standard by which it must be judged. The standard is clearly a moral one as this selection, again from Green, indicates:

The value then of the institutions of civil life lies in their operation as giving reality to these capacities of will and reason, and enabling them to be really exercised. In their general effect, apart from particular aberrations, they render it possible for a man to be freely determined by the idea of a possible satisfaction of himself, instead of being driven this way and that by external forces, and thus they give reality to the capacity called will: and they enable him to realize his reason (i.e., his idea of self-perfection) by acting as member of a social organization in which each contributes to the better-being of all the rest. So far as they do in fact thus operate they are morally justified, and may be said to correspond to the 'law of nature,' the jus naturae, according to the only sense in which that phrase can be intelligently used.[54]

This is a peculiar brand of idealism and it has implications which are not drawn from similar theories on the continent. The state is clearly a teleological category in these theories but it is also subservient to the aims of the individual. It does not assume responsibility for dictating moral interests but it does have a responsibility to allow these interests to flourish and to promote them wherever possible. In fact, it is social organization in general that aids individual moral goals and the state, particularly in the theories of G. D. H. Cole and Harold Laski, becomes only one of these organizations. And as the state was viewed from a moral standard, so was the man in society. Laski wrote that "each man is real to himself not by reason of the contacts he shares with his fellow man, but because he reaches those contacts through his own separate intellect and moral character."[55] There is an explicit ethical teleology at work here and it is to be found and nurtured through social institutions. The theory which emerged from this liberalism laid the theoretical foundation for the modern welfare state; politics was an affair for all men in which they searched for "the social good on the largest possible scale."[56] The last of the giants of English idealism, Ernest Barker, correctly defined political obligation on these terms as operative when the state promoted "the highest possible development of all the capacities of personality in all of [society's members]."[57]

Yet there is a paradox only barely buried beneath liberalism's new accommodation, and it emerges from its shallow grave when the problem of political obligation is confronted. For contrary to the spirit of liberalism, the state now stands *in loco parentis* to its citizenry. Since the state now assumes the responsibility for the moral development of its citizens, objections to political authority can be viewed as the objections of a frustrated child to be alternately overlooked and disciplined by the government. Even worse, if the state has not fulfilled its function in "promoting the development of the capacities of personality," then the dissident protests from the vantage point of a moral cretin, if only so out of neglect. Moral authority has been transferred from the citizenry to the state, quite against the wishes of the liberals who have conceived of politics in this fashion. It should not surprise us unduly, then, when the modern liberal who looks *sympathetically* at resistance movements uses a terminology of excuses. The rioter is more often than not viewed as a mistreated child, morally pure and worthy of our sympathy, but hardly an autonomous actor. Only illiberals can possibly evaluate resistance in terms of responsibility and moral decision.

The attempt of this essay, then, is to recapture what Lionel Trilling once called the "primal imagination of the liberal mind" and send it forth untarnished by accommodations with political action. The result, if readers accept the argument, is that the concept "political obligation," traditionally understood as embracing a moral imperative to obey political authority, has no place in a liberal society.

2

Moral Duty, Political Obligation, and the Doctrine of Conscience

By liberty I mean the assurance that every man shall be protected in doing what he believes his duty against the influence of authority and majorities, custom and opinion.

—*Lord Acton*

THERE IS A PASSAGE in John Locke's *Second Treatise* which has been sorely neglected. In his chapter on the dissolution of government Locke asks, "Who shall be Judge whether the Prince or Legislative act contrary to their Trust?"[1] Locke's answer, of course, has become conventional wisdom in liberal democratic political theory. He concludes that it is the people who shall be the judge:

The People shall be Judge; for who shall be Judge whether his Trustee or Deputy acts well, and according to the Trust reposed in him, but he who deputes him, and must, by having deputed him have still a Power to discard him, when he fails in his Trust? If this be reasonable in particular Cases of private Men, why should it be otherwise in that of the greatest moment; where the Welfare of Millions is concerned, and also where the evil, if not prevented, is greater, and the Redress very difficult, dear and dangerous?[2]

This, of course, is the Locke with whom we are all so familiar. The people are the "Proper Umpire." Who else? Where would all of us be without that reliable if pedantic Whig philosopher who can always be counted upon to appeal to our liberal sensibilities? Yet Locke's answer does not end there. A note of resignation follows:

> If the Prince or whoever they be in Administration, decline that way of Determination, the Appeal then lies no where but to Heaven. Force between either persons who have no known superior on earth, being properly a state of War, wherin the Appeal lies only to Heaven and in that state the injured Party must judge for himself, when he will think fit to make use of that Appeal, and put himself upon it.[3]

This is indeed an odd conclusion to a tract which for several hundred pages attempts to establish the need for government and offers a score of restraints that will keep it within bounds. In fact, part of the justification for liberal government for Locke lay in its tendency to resolve most conflict by accommodation rather than by force. Limited government, it is hoped, would allow men to follow their moral duty apart from the recourse to political action.[4] The appeal to heaven is traditionally seen as Locke's justification for the right of revolution. Yet it is barely a justification at all. Locke, in fact, falls silent at the threshold of revolution. The appeal to heaven is an announcement on Locke's part of the abdication of political philosophy before the barrel of a gun.

Locke's resignation has become lost to contemporary liberal democratic theory. For what Locke was saying was that political obligation could not ultimately be reconciled with moral duty, that there is a point when any government will say "you must withhold your judgment" and then go about enforcing its decision:

"For if [tyranny] reach no farther than some private Men's Cases, though they have a right to defend themselves, and to recover by force, that by unlawful force is taken from them; yet the Right to do so, will not easily engage them in a Contest, wherin they are sure to perish."[5] If we pay serious attention to Locke we will find that the moral claim of democrary is considerably weaker than we have been led to believe. It is a near universal belief that liberal democratic political systems leave room for the exercise of moral judgments since after all, caprice, the arch-villain of liberal theory, has been removed from politics. In classical liberal theory it is removed by limiting the scope of political action through constitutional restraints, in American pluralism by devising a system in which politics is managed at a low level of visibility through limited participation and reliance upon bargaining and compromise, in traditional conservatism by limitations upon majority rule and the social cushioning of custom, and in radicalism by combining moral sensitivity with political imagination. To the extent that the American political system exhibits all these features (or is thought to exhibit them), the subject of political obligation has an old-fashioned, if not a nonsensical ring.

Yet if we allow ourselves to appreciate the real genius of Locke, we will find that a political system, despite any or all of these contrivances, can still run counter to individual moral judgment. To account for this, Locke allowed for the reemergence of action by conscience despite his deep misgivings about its success. It is at this point that Locke and contemporary democratic theorists depart and it is at this point where I should like to begin.

The general aim of this chapter is to recapture the

liberal imagination by showing that doing one's moral duty and obeying political authority are inconsistent categories of action. We will carry this position to a conclusion rarely admitted by liberals in contending that no moral ground of political obligation is to be found. I hope to demonstrate this position by showing that there is a crucial distinction between the moral judgment (or decision) on the one hand and the moral principle on the other. Recent conceptions of moral duty have, I think, failed to appreciate this distinction and consequently have been unable to account for paradoxes when these theories are transposed to problems of political action. By way of establishing the significance of the moral judgment, it will be necessary to present a somewhat detailed analysis of the doctrine of conscience. I hope to show that the low standing of this doctrine in current political thought is less a reflection of its own ambiguities than the inherent failure of political action to seriously take account of it.

Ethical philosophy was the first academic discipline to move beyond the influence of positivism. In many ways the preoccupations of ethics today reflect this early departure. Its central questions remain: how are moral judgments justified? What moral principles can be applied to action? Yet ethical philosophers, in their concern with moving away from positivism, have lost sight of an important feature of metaethical discourse — the question of what sorts of considerations must be present for a moral judgment to be properly so called. Let me briefly mention some recent conceptions of morality to illustrate my point.[6] The earliest advances from the *de gustibus non disputandum* doctrine of ethics can be found in the writings of R. M. Hare and P. H. Nowell-Smith who, not surprisingly, emphasized the individual character of moral judgment. Both writers distinguished an ultimate justification of moral judgment from moral discourse in general. The former were indeed beyond meaningful discussion. The latter, however, were not. Hare indicates the point at which discussion ends:

If pressed to justify a decision completely, we have to give a complete specification of the way of life of which it is a part. . . . If the inquirer still goes on asking, 'But why should I live like that?' then there is no further answer to give him to make up his own mind which way he ought to live; for in the end everything rests upon a decision of principle. He has to decide whether to accept that way of life or not; if he accepts it, then we can proceed to justify the decisions that are based upon it; if he does not accept it, then let him accept some other, and try to live by it.[7]

Hare goes on to identify a set of formal conditions which distinguish the moral judgment from other sorts of judgments. It must be a decision based upon principle (Hare, it should be noted, is also writing against intuitionists as well as emotivists), and the principle must be one which the agent is willing to see applied to himself and others in like situations. Nowell-Smith is not as blunt as Hare but his position is similar, and perhaps for our purposes, more important:"The questions, 'What shall I do' and 'What moral principles should I adopt' must be answered by each man for himself; that at least is part of the connotation of the word 'moral.'"[8] The theories of Hare and Nowell-Smith are attitudinal approaches to ethics. Hare regards moral statements as imperatives, Nowell-Smith sees them as gerundives (incitements to action). Both hoped to show the logical relations among all attitudinal statements and attempted to mark off moral judgments by formal criteria. Yet in many respects these formal conditions failed to account for positions that affronted basic conceptions of morality. The judgments of the complete ethical egoist (one who pursues self-interest and allows others to do the same) and the fanatic seemed to fall under the requirements of the universalization principle.[9]

These were serious criticisms, and a number of new ethical theories were proposed to meet them. A major effort was directed at shifting attention and emphasis away from the individual autonomy of the moral judgment to a larger or more inclusive appeal. The new definition of morality moved away from the moral judgment and the attitudinal aspect of moral language to a requirement that demanded at least an appeal to social consensus. Morality was a social phenomenon, and as such, the moral judgment must take into consideration existing conceptions of moral rules. H. L. A. Hart has advanced a position that meets this focus yet still attempts to take into account the autonomous character of moral judgment. Clearly Hart's position deserves more consideration than it will receive here. For the moment, however, it should suffice to mention his concept of internal and external aspects of social rules. There are, of course, all sorts of social rules, some more general than others, some more widely followed than others, and some more crucial to the maintenance of social relationships than others. The latter are Hart's principal concern. He concludes that rules of this sort (rules, incidentally, which "characteristically involve sacrifice and renunciation") are the stuff of which morality is made. One's judgment is not moral then unless one claims some consensus of intersubjective duty in terms of social rules of obligation.[10] Furthermore, the moral character of a judgment is suspect if it does not meet the current consensus on social rules. Hart, however, refuses to conclude that those who do not accept the consensus on social rules are morally obliged. Moral duty is explained in the same terms as is attitudinal theory. Obligations arise only from the internal acceptance of social rules. They are dependent upon the recognition of obligations and are acts of individual will. Hart has rejected an attitudinal approach to the moral content of decisions by making them a function of the social group, yet he has kept the concept of moral duty within the boundaries of individual judgment.[11] This is a peculiar theory indeed, since it can place one in the position of doing one's moral duty as a result of a judgment that has been ruled by definition nonmoral. While it is certainly possible for one to think of cases in which a judgment of prudence creates a moral obligation, a definitional solution seems to be a most unsatisfactory method for containing them.

There is, however, a third concept of morality which moves even further from the notion that moral judgments are somehow dependent upon individual cognition. I am speaking of the "good reasons" theory of ethics. Stephen Toulmin, for instance, in his *An Examination of the Place of Reason in Ethics*, rejects attitudinal and intuitionist approaches to ethics as failing to take proper account of the process of moral reasoning. Toulmin suggests two sorts of reasoning. The first involves applying provisions of an existing moral code to a particular action. The second sort of reasoning concerns situations in which the application of a recognized moral code is not possible, as in the case of conflicting duties. Here the notion of social harmony must be the basis for the moral judgment: "What makes us call a judgment 'ethical' is the fact that it is used to harmonize people's actions."[12] Both kinds of reasoning described are moral (or good) since they both aim at "the harmony of society." For Toulmin, to question this point is to end the moral argument. If one questions why he should do "A" after the argument for social harmony has been presented, one can give no further moral reason at all, for he has come to the limit of morality.[13]

For all of Toulmin's attempt to move away from moral principles to moral reasoning, we find that he really has not traveled terribly far. Moral reasoning itself has been defined in terms of a moral principle (social harmony), and any reasoning which does not appeal to this moral principle is again, by definition, nonmoral reasoning. Toulmin's position becomes even more peculiar when one considers that moral reasoning frequently wreaks havoc with ongoing social structure. On Toulmin's terms we cannot call the judgments of Socrates, Christ, Beckett, and Gandhi "ethical." Moreover, moral judgment ends once the moral principle is questioned.

The effort to lead the consideration of moral "ought" statements away from an individual perspective toward broad social references has been a painstaking process. The hope has been that if one could validate judgments according to certain requirements of the social order, one could considerably broaden the arena of ethical philosophy. Yet I think this effort has been misguided in the sense that the process of reaching moral judgment has been subsumed under the consideration of the justification of moral principles. As the latter became more and more identified with material conditions and social goals, the moral judgment also became restricted.

This is a relatively subtle point but it is one which deserves careful consideration since it is directly relevant to the problem of political obligation. Let me approach the problem by talking about the statement "A promises B to do X and A keeps his promise to B at T_1." Normally ethical philosophers would be concerned with two basic questions here: Is it moral to keep promises? And what is the moral justification of promise-keeping? Yet there are another set of questions which can also be asked — what is A's justification for keeping promises and has A made a moral judgment in keeping a promise? These sets of questions appear to be quite similar and no doubt they are closely related. But there are differences. The first set asks about the rightness and wrongness of an action with a view toward assessing the moral worth of an individual who falls into this category. The second set, however, asks about the reasons why one acts with a view toward identifying kinds of reasons for acting. The former set of questions have to do with moral principles and the latter with moral judgment.

Let us run through some possible reasons which A might give for promise-keeping in order to clarify our above distinction. A may answer that (1) he keeps promises because his mother told him to do so; (2) he is just in the habit of keeping promises; (3) he keeps promises as a "rule of thumb;" (4) by doing so he is merely doing what he said he intended to do. Now none of these reasons for promise-keeping is morally repugnant to us. None of the responses directly evoke justifications of self-interest or mere compliance with sanctions. In fact, in the first case we might even conclude that A was a person of moral worth, particularly if he was blessed with a wise and virtuous mother. Yet a moral judgment has not been made in any of these cases despite the fact that in reasons two through four there are implications of appeals to social standards. All of these answers are the result of unexamined motives and unreflective thinking and as such are not examples of the exercise of moral judgment. In each case, A might have done an act of moral worth and this reasoning may even get him by with future acts deserving the same commendation.

What sorts of criteria, then, are inconsistent with the making of a moral judgment? I think we have already implied that to exercise moral judgment means that one has arrived at an assessment of action or a course of action itself by way of his own determination of what he ought to do. I am not going to say what sorts of formal conditions must be present for the moral judgment to be so-called apart from the restriction. Even the more sympathetic have concluded that formal conditions alone leave "too large a residue of substantive and moral variability."[14] Much of the problem dissolves, however, when we force ourselves to remember that the moral judgment per se need not be "right" to be called a moral judgment. And we can certainly say that this view of what the moral judgment entails eliminates action by habit or received tradition or a vague notion of social conformity. By keeping promises I may be acting according to a moral principle or I may be morally right but I have not made a moral judgment until by my own thoughts I have determined that I should keep this promise because I consider this the right course of action to take. We ourselves may conclude that it is moral to keep promises and that the moral justification of promises is, say, their social utility, but even though an agent mentions utility in keeping a promise, this in no way helps us conclude that he has exercised moral judgment. We do not know that he has exercised moral judgment until he tells us how he has arrived at the principle he has accepted. Now it should be made clear what I am not implying by moral judgment. I do not mean to suggest that by making a moral judgment and recognizing an attendant moral obligation I have necessarily acted morally or that any judgment cannot be criticized as faulty. But this becomes a question of arguing over moral principles reached by a moral judgment. Exercising moral judgment simply means considering what one ought to do and justifying that decision by reference to standards of action which he has chosen.[15] Attempts to identify moral judgments with material or group concerns, then, is not necessarily wholly inaccurate. What writers have failed to consider is that reference to these points must occur in a specific way for a moral judgment to occur; that is, they must be reached by individual determination. Now it is possible for a person's acts to be deserving of moral praise when he relies on what to do from the judgments of others. In this sense an assessment of moral worth or blame is independent of moral judgment. Yet reliance on habit or the opinion of others can also produce actions deserving of moral condemnation.[16] When a child justifies an action by saying, "Johnny said it was O.K.," we often reply by asking, "If Johnny said it was O.K. to jump in the river, would you do it?" What we are saying to the child is that advice and the giver must be carefully considered, which is another way of saying that one should decide for himself what he thinks is right. If making a moral judgment to act in a certain way makes one liable to error, reliance upon others or simple unreflective action certainly has its own liabilities.

I should now like to show how political action conflicts with the process of moral judgment and, while it still allows for assessing the moral worth of the state's actions, prevents the individual from meeting some very important moral obligations reached by moral judgment. In the concept of moral judgment which was just outlined, I avoided reference to the word "conscience." I have done so because current ethical philosophy has had a number of problems with this word, and I did not wish to confuse the point by introducing a potentially disruptive term. Now that the task of presenting the moral judgment is behind us, I think we are in a position to discuss what we might call "conscience-talk" (the justification of the decision of conscience, hereafter referred to as CT) in relation to the concept of moral judgment.

The doctrine of conscience has enjoyed an uneven popularity in the history of political and ethical thought. Political philosophers, for reasons that will become evident, have been particularly cautious in making use of the concept. When they have, it has been done in a framework that assured the reliability of the conscientious decision. That is, a political theorist who made use of the doctrine tended to do so when conscience could be formulated as the voice of God speaking to man. Yet, apart from some Reformation thinkers, theorists were still careful to limit its use since, although God's commands were morally infallible, some distortion seemed to result when these commands filtered through the frail ears of man. The theological employment of the concept of conscience, nevertheless, has had a significant impact on secular thought. For once the religious framework was vacated, serious problems followed, especially in terms of the justification of the judgment of conscience and the spatial location of its voice. A modest revision was offered by the Moral Sense philosophers in identifying conscience as a faculty of the mind. But it only kept its meaning within a particular moral and psychological theory that had problems of its own. Samuel Clarke was on the way toward offering a sensible secular reformulation of CT when modern science produced, in ever increasing waves of theory and evidence, a massive onslaught which, apart from a few clergymen and political dissidents, has eliminated conscience as a feature of moral discourse. Freudian psychology accounts for the "voice of conscience" by identifying CT with repressed desires. Behavioral psychology, expanding upon conscience's traditional moral connotation, views CT as expressing learned modes of reaction to stimuli. And most important for our purposes, moral philosophy, drawing upon anthropological and sociological explanation, has seen conscience in terms of the internalization of group norms.[17]

I will contend that the "appeal to conscience," or CT, is a legitimate way to express one's moral judgment, that once conscience is understood in terms of the process of moral judgment, many of the philosophical problems with the doctrine of conscience can be resolved. This discussion then will proceed in three parts — a consideration of fallacies about conscience (that is, unfounded objections to CT), a discussion of some genuine problems in the doctrine of conscience, and an attempt to move toward a consistent approach to CT.

One of the most common fallacies about a decision of conscience is that it is uncommunicable and hence unjustifiable (at least apart from the actual appeal) .[18] This position seems to be expressed in phrases like "this is a question of conscience" and, "my conscience has spoken and I can only act accordingly." If we accept the proposition of uncommunicability then the doctrine of conscience is clearly in trouble. For if I contend that I must do X or refrain from doing X and if such a judgment is bound to affect other individuals and if I have no means to communicate how or why I reached such a judgment except that my conscience said so, why should anyone take account of my position? Another has no way of knowing (at least in terms of asking me) whether my action is the result of self-interest or unfounded propositions or beliefs about others. I can insist that I do not do X not out of self-interest and that my judgment is indeed well-founded and correct; but if I am asked to explain myself or to respond to certain arguments to act differently and I say, "I will not be deterred, my conscience has spoken," what reason has another to accept my judgment? All he can do is assess my past actions, that is, consider my integrity and my consistency, and conclude that he will "respect my conscience." But then one has not really responded to an act of conscience as such but has responded to my past actions. My actions in past cases of nonconscientious decisions become the basis for respecting this particular act of conscience. The dilemma becomes more acute if my decision of conscience directly affects another and affects another to the detriment of his own moral or social position. All I can say is that I must punish him (by, say, ending our friendship) because he did something which my

conscience says is wrong. If he responds that all sorts
of reputable people do action X and do not consider it
wrong, I can respond that these people deserve my moral
condemnation also. If he pleads to be shown why he was
wrong so he can change his moral assessment of action
X in the future and repent his past act, all I can say is,
"Don't you have a conscience? Let it tell you what it
does me!" Now the other party may pretend to change
his ways out of the desire to keep my friendship without
actually seeing that he was wrong. But if he does, he
has destroyed his own moral autonomy, and if I con-
tinually appeal to acts of conscience in the future, I may
completely limit his recourse to (and perhaps his capacity
for) moral judgment. One may also try to talk with me
(and my conscience) by contending that I didn't think
that this action was wrong last week, but I can simply
reply that last week I hadn't consulted or followed or
listened to my conscience and that my conscience was
obscured or silenced by our friendship.

It is no wonder that recourse to conscience is laid
to rest in moral and political philosophy if indeed it
is so private and uncommunicable as our descussion
has suggested. But I do not think this need be so.
Decisions of conscience are susceptible to justification
and argumentation, and many of our expressions about
conscience indicate that this is so. Let us look at the
expression, "My conscience has spoken and I can only
act accordingly." We have so far taken this statement
to mean "Don't talk to me about this anymore — I will
not listen to your arguments." We assume that when
one is "listening" to his conscience, and when that conscience has indeed spoken, that this mysterious faculty
prevents its holder from hearing any outside discourse.
Conscience, at least at this point, is the most demand-

ing of tyrants. It "bothers," "leads," and even "torments" its holder, even when he might — if he were not so possessed — wish to place it in some dark corner and forget about it. There is a paradox here of significant proportions. We tell people to "follow their consciences," rebuke those who "have no conscience," yet once that little devil (or more properly, angel) is activated, he knows no mercy. He cuts us apart from discourse with other men and allows us to listen only to voices within our own mind. Conscience is at once cruelly active and quite passive, revered and respected by men despite the fact that it creates the most headstrong fanatics. Conscience never talks to us with a sweet melodious voice; when it does speak it is always monotonous and nagging. Only by the most exacting demands is it silenced.

But there is a way out. Yet the rejection of the possibility of CT will not do it, since we are still faced with the doctrine of conscience. We simply will not give up the notion that, however torturous and nagging, the voice of conscience should be listened to. But the expressions "It's a question of conscience" and "My conscience has spoken and I can only act accordingly" can mean other things. When I say to another, "It's a question of conscience," I am saying to him that I cannot make this decision for him, that he must do what he thinks is morally right. This need not mean that there is no advice or rule to be offered in this situation and that one must search the recesses of his mind for what is essentially a "private" and uncommunicable decision. Seeking a conscientious decision then can be a very public act, that is, an act characterized by moral argumentation and discussion with others. The expression "It is a question of conscience" can be a distinguishing statement from another point of view. One can ask me why I did action X. The action was not legally required of me, nor did anyone expect or depend upon me to do X. My response would be that "it was a question of conscience," and by making use of this phrase I am saying that I considered this a *moral* question and hence applied *moral* standards to my decision to take action X. In other words, I have used the doctrine of conscience, or at least referred to it, to explain that I have made a moral judgment.

Conscience then both suggests a process and assigns certain considerations in terms of that process. By saying that "my conscience is bothering me," I am saying that I do not know what to do or that I do not know if what I did was right. I am weighing moral considerations against considerations of another sort; I am weighing moral ought statements against other sorts of oughts. Conscience represents the consideration of those former kind of statements. To say that "I couldn't with good conscience do that" is to say that I have moral objections against doing or countenancing an action and that I am bound to live by these considerations. To advise that one's conscience should be one's guide is to offer a particular kind of advice, an advice which says two things: think about moral considerations in your judgment and come to terms with these considerations yourself. It need not provoke withdrawing into a private discourse never to come out again. It only demands individual consideration of the moral consequences of actions. To contend that this sort of judgment is uncommunicable is to add a particular moral epistemology to CT. It is not part of the idea of conscience itself, and our everyday language does not suggest any epistemology which would destroy it. To say "If only you would heed your conscience, you would see (that X is the action to take)" is a plea to consider the moral implications of an action. But it is a plea, not a command, for conscience cannot be *ordered* up by authority or produced by acquiescence or coercion. One can ask that another heed or follow or consult conscience. But to deal in CT is to exercise moral judgment; no one can do that for another.

We have concluded that to reach a decision of conscience is to reach a moral judgment, but that is not to say that the decision is uncommunicable. A weaker form of this charge is the position that decisions of conscience are decisions somehow necessarily apart from moral rules.[19] Conscience here is linked to an intuitionist ethic and as such suffers, not only from inadequacies in justification, but from inadequacies in terms of persuasion. This also, I think, is a mistaken position and, like our first fallacy, is the result of misinterpretations of certain expressions about conscience. We may say, for instance, "My conscience says I can't do that." The inference here is that a certain action would be the wrong action to take. At this point conscience does appear to be solely act-oriented. An act is somehow inherently wrong and the appeal to conscience, like a divine finger of accusation, is its own justification. This version of conscience was a predominant feature of the early days of the New Left movement. Mario Savio contended that "if some issue of fact about our society does not arouse deep feeling on its own merits, then either we are lacking in moral sensitivity, or the issue is unworthy of deep feeling. . . . I have a deep-seated suspicion of anyone who requires a theory to show that some practice is morally wrong."[20] Savio's alternatives seem to be accepted by those who followed him and who indeed have concluded that America "lacks moral sensitivity." Posing alternatives such as this has, I think, been unfortunate and is characteristic of all ethical theories based upon self-evidence. One either agrees or is quickly accused of wrong thinking, or worse. Yet to say, "My conscience says I can't do that," need not indicate that I necessarily operate in an ethics void of rules or principles. I can say that my own considered moral judgment is that "all actions which violate human life" are wrong. It is this principle, the result of a decision of conscience, to which I adhere. In fact, many would contend that those who employ CT as a basis for refraining from certain actions mistakenly select principles of too great a generality, considering the complexities of life around them. The conscientious objector to war is often accused of principled behavior beyond necessity or expectation. (This criticism leads to our next fallacy, however, so we will hold further comment here.)

The doctrine of conscience is inclusive enough to hold nearly any moral principle. One may base his actions upon, say, utility and invoke an appeal to conscience. I could say, for instance, that "the reason I am a Democrat is that I have a conscience" and go on to explain that this particular party promotes policies benefitting the majority of the citizenry, rather than those policies which would benefit only a few. What I am saying is that I consider moral rules important (if not overriding) and that this party promotes the moral rule of utility, a rule to which I subscribe. It does not sound odd for me to invoke conscience and speak of moral rules. Only by misconstruing the intermittency of appeals to conscience as the result of flashes of intuition rather than as one's assignment of precedence to other considerations can we conceive of CT as standing in opposition to justification with reference to moral rules.

The third and final fallacy to which I should like to speak is one that pictures CT as an arrogant, self-righteous position which, while perhaps different in motivation from the pursuance of personal gain, nevertheless is the same in the sense that it ignores the interests and needs of other men. The decision of conscience is reached by a consideration of one's own beliefs alone; those of others are pushed aside and discarded. This view of conscience is also closely related to our first fallacy: that is, the fallacy of overprivatizing CT. Its emphasis, however, is more straightforward — for to view the exercise of conscience as moral arrogance is to directly question an individual's capacity to exercise his moral judgment and, perhaps more importantly, to question the desirability of having recourse to it.[21] Conscience-talk becomes associated with stubbornness, intractability to compromise, intolerance, and the assertion of possession of absolute truth — all of which are dispositions generally frowned upon in democratic theory. Again I submit that this is clearly not so: in fact, CT and decisions of conscience are probably less likely to be self-righteous than other sorts of discourse and decisions. This assertion, in fact, has already been questioned in our discussion of the second fallacy. The statement, "Here I stand — I can do no other," appears at the end of a discourse over moral judgment and not at its beginning. Yet, I should like to consider several additional points which appear to be linked to the notion that decisions of conscience are decisions of self-righteousness. More than one philosopher has been concerned with this question, but I will devote myself to a discussion by H. D. Lewis. Lewis's position is noteworthy in that he tries to approach this fallacy head on and in systematic fashion. And perhaps more importantly, he is not unsympathetic to the appeal of conscience and the possibility of CT. Lewis begins by noting that "while the individual must in the last analysis obey his own conscience, yet, as part of his duty to find out what is his duty, there is much in the meantime that he requires to do to correct the limitations of his private points of view."[22] This statement is of considerable importance, for if it can be advanced that the decision of conscience allows for the views of others and perhaps, as Lewis suggests, *requires* such considerations, the charge against CT of self-righteousness, at least as a blanket rebuttal, is unfounded. Our problem, however, is a bit more complicated. For if a conscientious decision involves taking into consideration the positions of others, we must at some point decide whether a decision of conscience has indeed been made or whether a decision of conscience has actually been made on the basis of reliance upon others in terms of some recognized authority or of prudence. That is, if taking account of the positions of others occurs in some specific ways, we may well be forced to ask if indeed moral judgment has been exercised at all. The point at which CT takes account of others and still remains CT is a sticky problem but I think we will find that it is not merely a question of degree and that we can with reasonable assurance find that point, a point which, of course, includes some consultation with and consideration of others.

This is precisely what Lewis did. But alas, I think he has thrown the net too wide. He suggests four major areas which the conscientious decision-maker should take into consideration in order to avoid the charge of self-righteousness:

A. We can hardly discover our duty independently of what has been taught about the matter by others. Principles that are widely acknowledged and have persisted through many changes deserve special respect.

B. Regard for the opinion of others has a further form arising especially from the fact that much that is relevant to ethical decisions is not accessible to each individual. . . . Deference to the judgment of others has a wide application outside the strictly ethical field. . . . But there is a widespread tendency to make an exception of ethics, regardless of the fact, not merely that we are variously endowed with ethical insight, but also that those who know the facts best must also, to a great extent, evaluate them for us.

C. [It is] . . . meaningful, in some circumstances, to affirm that we ought to act as other persons think we ought to act even when we are assured that these others are mistaken and our own opinions sound; the 'weaker brother' has to be considered.

D. The course which our ethical judgment suggests in regard to the general nature of a situation may require to be modified in the light of the procedure adopted by others, whether or not this procedure is prompted by ethical considerations. . . . A surgeon, for example, may find himself committed to assist at an operation which he would not recommend himself.[23]

I would not deny that all four of these considerations raise important ethical problems and that it is possible to say that an individual "ought" to act on the basis of these principles in various situations. What I am concerned with, however, is the question of the extent to which these principles are consistent with the making of conscientious decisions. Considerations raised in A and certain interpretations of C and D are, I think, consistent with the requirements of conscientious decisions. B clearly is not, and to use the appeal to conscience in this context is not only inconsistent with our notions of CT but is, I would contend, quite untoward in terms of our ordinary language. The consideration of existing ethical principles is far from inconsistent with the conscientious decision. Exercising and acting upon one's moral judgment is both a very difficult and a serious matter. Moral rules can provide help to the conscientious individual in a variety of ways. He may use them to consider what he ought to do in a situation about which he is confused. That is, if when one "consults" his conscience he is asking himself what course of moral action to take, a consideration of moral principles may give a keener insight into the consequences of his actions. Moral rules also provide one who appeals to conscience with a justification for a decision, or more precisely, a bridge between his decision to act and a reason for others to approach conscientiously what they also ought to do. But we must emphasize that the decision of conscience can challenge certain existing ethical principles as well as invoke them. If this possibility is not recognized, we have transferred the moral judgment into simple obedience to current ethical standards of conduct. Such moral standards may be considered, but to give them such weight that they must be accepted prima facie is to move from CT to other sorts of discourse. More frequently than not, however, the charge against those who appeal to conscience is that the moral principle which has been invoked deserves an exception. The basis for that exception is usually a nonmoral standard. The rejoinder to the charge that CT is self-righteous is really to say that the decision of conscience gives priority to moral courses of action. But while certain situations may require duties other than moral ones, we would hardly describe as arrogant a position which demanded that the burden of argument rest with those who call for adoption of nonmoral standards.

A rebuttal to all the implications of the position offered by H. D. Lewis in B is impossible. This is an argument based upon an ethical epistemology which is beyond our current discussion. But we can say this much. No one would deny that the capacity for moral sensitivity is uneven in men. Differences in native intelligence, education, social class, and personal disposition all contribute to varying degrees of ethical insight. Yet the question we must ask is this: are these differences great enough to justify reliance upon others for moral courses of action? Are they great enough, to put it in another way, to justify the abrogation of moral judgment? I think not, at least in terms of an across-the-board reliance, and it is only this blanket position which calls for rejection of an appeal to conscience for large portions of a population for most of their decisions. We also must ask to what extent it makes sense to demand reliance upon "moral experts" when one becomes such an expert by virtue of the fixed advantages of a social structure. While ethics is not "learned" in the same way as mathematics, the whole pattern and quality of life that a "moral education" promotes is, indeed, part of a society's distribution of goods. In fact, it may be possible for one, at some point, to say: "Yes, your comprehension of the subtleties of moral discourse is in no way comparable to mine, but who is responsible for my crudity in terms of moral sensitivity but the social system which allowed you, and not me, to become a moral authority?" At this point, the best response of the moral expert may be to say: "Yes, despite the fact that deference to my position may result in the best course of moral action, you are entitled to the exercise of your own moral judgment." If the position in C is interpreted in this sense, I think it is relevant to the conscientious decision. 24

As important as the above position is, we must face

Lewis's contention head on: is deference to the moral expert an exercise of conscience? I think not, and a brief look at the way CT is used can justify my position. Jones has not seen Smith for some time and he asks him what he eventually did about a particular moral dilemma he was in. Smith replies: "My conscience told me to follow whatever Aristotle said" or "I followed my conscience and decided to do whatever Aristotle said about the matter." Now this would surely strike Jones as a very convoluted use of the word "conscience." He might ask, "How did you know that what Aristotle said would be consistent with your conscience?" Smith would respond: "Because I acknowledged Aristotle as a binding moral authority." There is no way to escape the odd sound that the appeal to conscience has in this context. Jones must conclude that Smith does not understand what a decision of conscience means. Nevertheless there is a way in which the teachings of Aristotle can be relevant to this sort of decision, and this way goes far toward striking at the heart of the claim that actions of conscience are self-righteous. Smith could have said: "I read Aristotle that night and he aroused my conscience, so I decided to do X" or "I didn't know what to do so I sat down and read Aristotle, whom I recognize as a man of considerable wisdom; I decided that his position was the right course of action to take, so I did X." There is a very important difference between letting others influence one's actions (first response) or consulting others (second response) and relying upon others in order to do what is morally right. The difference lies between the exercise of conscience and deference to the moral judgment of others.

The argument offered in D is an interesting one but I think we must consider at least two important factors,

or else we will end up again unduly restricting conscience, or worse yet, leading ourselves into countenancing
unspeakable practices. Submitting to the decisions of
others appears justifiable when the procedure decided
upon is largely a "question of judgment" (in the sense
that when a number of choices with relatively slight
differences exist and when it is not reasonable to quarrel
over the choice of any one of them we may call our choice
a question of judgment). It is also justifiable in areas
in which procedures have little effect upon the lives
and basic values of others, as in the case of deciding
whether the red on a traffic light should last one or two
minutes. Lewis's example of the surgeon participating
in an operation which he would not recommend approaches a borderline and as such deserves some consideration. Certainly it is possible to contend that if the
doctor thought the operation was dangerous and unnecessary, he should appeal to his chief of staff or his
medical association. Likewise, we would hardly approve
of a doctor who participated in those Nazi concentration
camp operations on the basis that he was required to
modify his moral judgment "in light of the procedure
adopted by others."

I think we can safely say, then, that the situations
falling under category D do require the revision of one's
moral judgment but they are not the stuff that great
moral predicaments are made of. The most that we might
claim from Lewis's observation is that the exercise of
conscience is not to be taken lightly and invoked on all
occasions accompanied by group decisions. Given the
considerable sanctions (both formal and informal) which
may be placed upon one who says, "Wait, I simply cannot
approve of that!" we are not on shaky ground when
we say that a restriction based upon some criterion of

importance be left to the dissenter. But Lewis does lose
sight of his subject at this point and leaves behind almost
all of his previous notions of what an appeal to conscience
entails. He deduces the following from his position in
D: "Where our convictions come into conflict with the
requirements of the state it is normally our duty to submit
to the state. The judge, for example, does not follow
his private opinion of the matter before him."[25] There
is an important difference, however, between the individual as a judge (or as any governmental official)
and the individual as a moral agent. We allow for certain
social roles which do not require a process of moral
judgment. Yet there are times when even these roles
are not adequate to justify an action or decision. The
rules which one is required to follow in occupying a
specified social role are the basis for one sort of
judgment, but they clearly are not the basis for judgments
of conscience. Nowell-Smith's remarks on the moral
decision can impress our point: "A moral decision is
a decision to act on a principle that one freely accepts,
not a decision to act on a principle on which one is told
to act."[26] This is a position far from self-righteousness,
unless one insists that making a moral judgment itself
is a self-righteous act. Few of us would admit the latter.

I think we have now disposed of a number of the most
common objections to a doctrine of conscience and by
doing so, we have gone far toward establishing something
approaching a consistent conscience talk. There remain,
however, a number of serious problems with the doctrine
of conscience before we can finish our task. Yet I think
we will find that, while these problems are not
philosophically resolvable, at least in terms of the doctrine of conscience, they are problems which we can
manage to live with.

Our first problem may have already been anticipated by the careful reader. It is, simply stated, that the grammar of CT is systematically ambiguous about who and with what forces and authority, is actually speaking. On the one hand, conscience appears to represent the agent's moral judgment or his process of moral judgment. We frequently say, "This is a question of conscience," meaning, as we have already noted, that one must exercise his own moral judgment in this case. We also talk about having conscientious objections to an action when we mean to suggest that our introspection on a particular matter has led to certain conclusions about how to or how not to act. But we also say, and without any apparent hesitation, that my "conscience has spoken," "my conscience has been bothering me," "I am forced by my conscience." To make matters worse we also say, again without any puzzlement on the part of the listener, "Let your conscience be your guide," "consult," "heed," "follow," and "listen to" the conscience. We appeal to others' consciences ("If you would only listen to your conscience, you would see . . . ," "Have you no conscience?," "How can you with good conscience do that?"). There are at least two problems here. First, is conscience the speaker or is it somehow separate from the speaker? And second, if conscience is somehow separate from the speaker, does it speak, using Nowell-Smith's terminology, as a judge or as an advocate?[27] In the first case we are asking if conscience is somehow prior to our convictions to act or if it represents one of our dispositions to act.

In ages with different world views the notion of conscience separate from the speaker presented no problems. In fact, by speaking of conscience in this manner one could reinforce current religious doctrines. Men, left to their own inclinations, may be disposed to act in certain rather uniform directions, but conscience, either as scriptures implanted by God or as the voice of God Himself, indeed *forces* one to act differently.[28] This may have been a reason why conscience often assumes the role of a judge. What the doctrine of conscience still means, however, is that one can possess a moral sensibility and that this sensibility to invoke conscience or to make a semioperative statement about conscience such as "My conscience has been bothering me" is to say that I have considered the moral implications of an act which have led me to do this rather than that or, at least, to hesitate doing this. To refer to conscience as a thing as we do when we say "my conscience" is a way of stating one's existing moral dispositions, say, in regard to killing or stealing or gossiping. To refer to conscience as a process as in "My conscience is bothering me" is to say that one either is in the throes of conflicting dispositions to act or is thinking through the moral consequences to an action. Conscience may sound more like a judge when existing moral dispositions are strong and directly apply to a particular situation and more like an advocate when the morally correct course is not clear or when strong nonmoral considerations bear upon a decision to act.

It is not a case of sloppy language or confused philosophy, then, to say that conscience is both a faculty and a process, a judge and an advocate, as long as we recognize that the faculty of which we speak has no spatial reference and that the judge is only our own dispositions speaking and not some "other" voice. These are difficult revisions to live with since the language of conscience tends to push us toward a literal interpretation of its grammar. But the fact of the matter is that we have no other way of expressing all the things about conscience-talk which we have discussed without utilizing the doctrine of conscience. Only by the doctrine of conscience can we emphasize the nature of moral judgment as an individually autonomous process and decision. We cannot say, "This bothers your conscience."[29] In using the doctrine of conscience we force ourselves to be reminded of the nature of moral judgment (and perhaps of morality in general) as a necessarily self-enforcing, rational exercise. The most we can manage and remain consistent with the demands of language is, "Doesn't that bother *your* conscience?" or "That would bother *my* conscience." The grammar of conscience, despite the trappings which it holds out for us, expresses a very plain and central truth. We may never be capable of living by it or constructing a society which can meet it, but to ignore it is to risk losing our moral sensibilities (individually or collectively) entirely.

The second major problem with the doctrine of conscience to which I should like to speak does not revolve about question of grammar, or to put it in another way, does not arise from the doctrine of conscience itself. This is the problem of the relation between a decision of conscience and moral rightness. We have admitted that we have no assurance that moral judgments will be correct ones. But we have also contended that decisions reached by other methods can also make no claim to infallibility. We have also seen that the statement, "Always let your conscience be your guide," need not be a claim to the moral infallibility of conscience but only a claim for the desirability of making moral judgment or for a consideration of the moral implications of actions. But let us at this point talk about the doctrine in terms of moral rightness. The advice, "Always let your conscience be your guide," or in stronger form,

"Do what your conscience tells you," can convey two related but different meanings. It can mean your conscience is always right; that is, your moral judgment is morally infallible. Or it can mean always do what you think is right. In the latter, we have not moved too far away from the meaning which claims only the desirability of making and acting upon one's moral judgments. Now we can say that the former, the position which claims moral infallibility in regard to decisions of conscience, is much too broad a piece of advice. We can think of all sorts of situations in which moral judgment undertaken by the most sensitive of persons is liable to err. Yet the advice that one should do what he thinks is right can be considered sensible advice if we take it to be *a claim.* By a claim, I mean the presumption that a decision of conscience should be acted upon. This means that the burden of proof lies with others (once the decision has been explained) in establishing that this claim shall not be respected. This seems to be the only reasonable course to take if we assume that "always do what you think is right" means something more than merely "never do what you thing is wrong"; that is, if we take "always do what you think is right" to mean a claim to the desirability of making moral judgment. If, as Nowell-Smith has suggested, part of the connotation of the word "moral" involves letting each man himself answer "What shall I do?" we should take the risk of the fallibility of moral judgments, especially if we admit the fallibility of nonmoral judgments.

But there is much more to say about the relation between decisions of conscience and moral rightness than to assert the general desirability of undertaking moral judgment. I think that if we apply some of the lessons we have learned about CT from our discussions of fallacies about the doctrine of conscience we will find that much, though not all, of the concern about the rightness of action based upon conscience falls by the wayside. Consider the following statement by Gen. Hershey, former director of the selective service: "If one person has the right to burn his draft card because his conscience says he must, then another fellow has the right to shoot somebody because his conscience works a little differently, and you just get into all sorts of things!"[30] The general is quite right in saying that one gets into all sorts of things. But he is clearly wrong in assuming that providing for and acceding to an invocation of conscience requires one to accede either on the basis of the appeal itself (that is, by just hearing the word "conscience!") or to not accede at all. Gen. Hershey's comment was chosen only because it presents a caricature of a widely held position. Therefore, I should now like to show, by way of repeating our earlier arguments, that this position is unfounded. On the basis of our previous discussion I would now like to present five necessary requirements for an appeal to conscience to be considered legitimate. We shall find that these requirements go far toward accounting for moral fallibility, perhaps further than do other sorts of decisions. I think we shall also find that all governments, including democratic ones, have nonetheless failed to allow for the "inviolability" and "sanctity" of conscience on these grounds.

I present little in the way of commentary on these requirements since they are really only a condensation of our critical discussion on fallacies about conscience. In the appeal to conscience an agent must:

1. Demonstrate that his act is a result of individual moral judgment. That is, the agent must show that his decision to act is based upon his own considered answer to the question, "What must I do?"

2. Demonstrate the basis of his decision. This may include reference to a moral principle; the influence of relevant "authorities," or even in some cases a style or pattern of life.

3. Demonstrate that he has considered the consequences of his actions, both moral and nonmoral, direct and indirect.

4. Advocate that others commit themselves to the *process* of moral judgment described in 1. The word "process" is emphasized here, for an agent who reaches a decision by way of conscience and evokes the doctrine of conscience as a justification for his act can demand no more than the same sort of *search* for moral considerations on the part of others.

5. State a willingness to defend his positions in 2 and 3 and to reconsider them on the basis of new information or arguments.

Now none of these five points are "tacked onto" or even "congenial" to the doctrine of conscience; they *are* the doctrine of conscience and the sort of CT which it allows. The four points beyond the demand that a moral judgment be made all take into account moral fallibility and provide for an elimination, as much as possible, of its risks. Can we say as much for decisions to act based upon tradition or upon reliance on others or upon authority?

The application of all this discussion to the moral obligation of a citizen to a liberal democratic system is direct and incurably damaging. I should like to approach this whole problem through a very brief mention of one of the central ethical justifications of liberal democracy (one which Locke appears to have accepted). Its argument goes something like this. Men are equal in their capacity to make correct moral judgments. They, of course, are also equal in respect to their capacity to err in making these judgments. The practices of universal franchise and majority rule are ways of realizing this equal capacity to make correct ethical decisions within a framework of moral fallibility. These practices become the only way in which one can recognize and make account for both of these assertions. Yet when one exercises moral judgment and comes to a conscientious decision in dissent from the majority, the government now, in the name of the represented (or worse, in the name of its own moral expertise), asserts in effect its moral infallibility by refusing to respect the claims of the conscientious agent. Liberal democracy then always fails to recognize the principle from which the justification for its authority was intended.

This is not to say that the most enlightened of democratic governments have left the matter to stand exactly as we have described it. They have not been entirely insensitive to the position of the conscientious dissenter. After all, phrases like the "right of conscience," the "inviolability of conscience," the "sanctity of conscience" are rarely absent from either democratic texts or policy-makers' speeches. Yet the way in which these governments have attempted to obviate the dilemma of acceding to an individual judgment of conscience while at the same time justifying political authority is such that the "right of conscience" is never respected in any meaningful sense.

Let me illustrate this point by way of a brief discussion of the issue of conscientious objection to military service. This, of course, is an extremely complicated problem and one whose immediate import in America has been diminished by the current experiment with a volunteer army, but I intend to confine my remarks to the opinions of the report of the National Advisory Commission on Selective Service (Marshall Commission) on the subject.[32] The Marshall Commission report is a particularly valuable document for the political theorist because it makes an attempt to justify a particular policy according to literal democratic theory. The Commission was divided on the issue of conscientious objection to conscription. While the majority and the minority of the panel offer different arguments for their positions, I think we shall find that the positions themselves and their justifications are not terribly different.

The question before the Marshall Commission was whether it should recommend changes in congressional legislation concerning conscientious objection. Congress had laid down three basic criteria to determine eligibility for this status. The registrant must: (1) base his objections on *religious* training and belief; (2) demonstrate that his objections are conscientious (i.e., *sincerely* held as binding in conscience) ; (3) object to war in any form. Religious belief was defined as a belief in man's relation to a supreme being that involved duties superior to those arising from among men. It expressly excluded beliefs which are essentially "political, sociological, philosophical" or of a "personal moral code." In 1965 the Supreme Court revised this definition to conclude "a given belief that is sincere and meaningful [and] occupies a place in the life of its possessor parallel to that filled by the orthodox belief in God is one which clearly qualifies for the exemption."[33] The result of this legislation was to produce, even with the judicial revision, a serious inconsistency. First Congress contended that it would not consider the merit of the conscientious decision but nevertheless would respect that decision if it were sincerely held. Then, however, Congress went on to demand substantive requirements for the conscientious decision.

The majority of the Commission supported current legislation on this point. Its arguments are noteworthy, if incorrect. Its first point is that "the question of 'classical Christian doctrine' on the subject of just and unjust wars is one which would be interpreted in different ways by different Christian denominations and this is not a matter upon which the Commission could pass judgment (p. 50)." But the Commission has clearly already passed judgment by contending that current religious positions on this issue are inconclusive and consequently ruled out as a legitimate defense for a decision of conscience. The Commission has committed the error of confusing moral judgment with moral principles. In respecting certain moral principles it contends that it has upheld the right of moral judgment. What is has really done is to respect only those moral judgments which arrive at the moral principles it accepts.

The Commission's second argument is perhaps the most prevalent justification of obedience to democratic government. We shall find, however, that on the basis of our previous discussion it is the most inconsistent and weakest of all possible arguments. We are told that "so-called selective pacifism is essentially a political question of support or nonsupport of a war and cannot be judged in terms of special moral imperatives. Political opposition to a particular war should be expressed through recognized democratic processes and should claim no special right of exemption from democratic decisions." Two related claims have been made here: (1) opposition to a war is not a moral but a "political" decision and (2) as a political decision it is subject to obligation by majority rule. Unfortunately this is a facile resolution to a very serious problem. The dissenter has already based his decision upon an appeal to conscience, which makes it prima facie a moral claim. And if the dissenter has met the requirements of a conscientious decision which we have outlined, he presumably has stated why he considered his claim to be a moral one. Certainly the Commission would not have the state define what is a moral claim and what is not. And even if it could do so, the Commission has already conceded that there is some moral status to conscientious objection by noting the Christian distinction between just and unjust wars. The whole matter is put on even worse footing when the Commission in its fourth argument justifies refusing recognition to selective conscientious objection on the basis of an inconsistency in the dissenter's *moral* claim: "The Commission was unable to see the morality of a proposition which would permit the selective pacifist to avoid combat service by performing noncombatant service in support of a war which he had theoretically concluded to be unjust" (p. 49). The remaining two points of the majority of the Marshall Commission involve consideration of alleged consequences (moral and nonmoral) of respecting this form of conscientious dissent. They include the contention that legal recognition "could quickly tear down the fabric of government" and "could be disruptive to the morale and effectiveness of the Armed Forces." We have said that this form of argument against one who makes a decision of conscience is legitimate. It would remain for the dissenter to answer these objections. But the Commissions's explanation of the latter argument deserves our own response. The majority contends:

A determination of the justness or unjustness of any war could only be made within the context of that war itself. Forcing the necessity of making that distinction — which would be the practical effect of taking away the government's obligation of making it for him — could put a burden heretofore unknown on the man in uniform and even on the brink of combat, with results that could well be disastrous to him, to his unit and to the entire military tradition (p. 49).

The Commission, by contending that a conscientious decision against a war must take place in combat conditions only, has again sought an easy resolution to the problem. It has mixed that contention with the frank assertion that moral judgment rests with the state. The Commission never faced up to the fact that moral judgment is suspended by political authority even in noncombat conditions.

We have noted that there was a minority view on the Marshall Commission. The position of this part of the panel is most instructive. It states with considerable candor and forthrightness the argument we are attempting to present:

Although the decision to make war is the prerogative of a duly constituted government, responsible to its people, and constitutes a presumption for the citizen in favor of the legitimacy of the war, the citizen still is personally responsible for his own moral judgments on matters of public policy. He may not abdicate his own conscience into the hands of government. In making his moral judgment on the legitimacy of war he must assess the political and military factors in the case, but the judgment itself is to be a moral judgment. In particular cases, therefore, it can happen that the conscientious moral judgment of the citizen is in conflict with the judgments made by government, either with regard to the justice of the nation's cause or with regard to the measure and mode in which military force is to be employed in the defense of the nation's vital interests. In such cases the citizen should not be compelled by government to act against his conscience by being forced to bear arms (p. 49).

The minority proposes that "the objector should be obliged to state his case before a competent panel." This is entirely consistent with the doctrine of conscience we have presented. The minority indicates a view of conscience quite similar to what we have suggested: "Young men would be required to reflect on the issues of war and peace, under the guidance of their mentors, and thus enabled properly to form their consciences at an early age." (p. 49).

But, alas, the recommendations ultimately fail to allow moral judgment to remain consistent with the demands of political authority. The minority contends that the purpose "would not be to judge whether he was right in his assessment of the political, military and moral values in the situation, but simply to convince his judges that his objection was 'truly held,' in the words of the Seeger decision" (p. 49). Furthermore, this report makes a distinction between "responsible students who feel caught in a dilemma, namely, between their duty to their country and what they see as the exigencies of personal integrity and conscience" and "a handful of irresponsible individuals whose opposition to particular wars is simply part of a broader revolt against organized society." The former group "deserves serious consideration"; the latter "should be deprived of an issue which gives them an opportunity of seeming to represent all opposition." Now, either sincerity is considered here to be in some way related to the extent of opposition to the state, in which case the panel is saying one cannot be sincere and still express extensive opposition to society as presently organized, or the doctrine of conscience is only to be respected to the extent to which one's conscience supports, in large part, existing political authority. In either case the axe of political authority falls upon the exercise of conscience.

What we have seen by examining the arguments of the Marshall Commission in the area of conscientious objection is that the exercise of political authority is simply incompatible with the exercise of conscience. The exercise of moral judgment is quite different from the acceptance of political authority. In the former, recognition of duty is based upon an autonomous decision to do what is right; in the latter, recognition of duty is subsequent to state determination of what is right. While moral judgments may lead one to support political authority, they can also lead one to oppose it. When the latter occurs the state is simply not in a position to respect moral judgment. The most it can do is devise criteria for recognition of the claims of conscience. Yet these criteria are designed to place decisions of conscience in a context so wide as to prevent moral discourse. Recognition of the intensity or sincerity of beliefs excuses a citizen from performance of a particular duty without benefit of consideration of the merit of the moral judgment. The state excuses its dissenters from participation in governmental policies while it goes on to resolve the moral dispute according to its own determination. After all, an action is no less wrong because you have been permitted to abstain from participating in it. Should the government, however, decide to consider the merit of a decision of conscience (in the spirit of the five points offered above), it becomes the judge, jury, and prosecutor in the dialogue.

The likelihood of the "inviolability of conscience" established as a result of a discourse between an individual and the state is terribly remote. Locke was well aware of this. His "Appeal to Heaven" was a recognition of the futility of conscience-talk in the face of political authority. Yet somehow Locke's sobriety faded in the face of more enthusiastic liberals who contended that the intersection between morality and politics would be achieved by the application of greater ingenuity.

The fact we must confront is that moral judgment and morality are self-enforcing activities; political authority and political action are not. The traditional political philosophers were aware that there is a basic and unresolvable dilemma here. One of the functions of the "state of nature" was to represent the abrogation of moral judgment by political authority as voluntary. They (Locke among them) sought to demonstrate how one could have a moral duty to the state apart from the self-legislation of individual moral judgment. That, of course, is another story. But the moral claim of political authority may not fare any better in that drama either.

3

The Liberal Myth:
The Consent Model

Yes, it is the same dusty idol, scarred and cracked by
the lance of Hume, battered by the Historical School,
mocked by every schoolboy who knows he didn't sign
a Contract. But we bow to it every time we demand the
"consent of the governed" and denounce the exercise of
hower beyond authority.

—*Joseph Tussmann*

I bid adieu to the social contract: and I left it to those
to amuse themselves with this rattle, who could think
they needed it.

—*Jeremy Bentham*

THEORIES OF JUSTICE, utility, tradition, divine right,
gratitude, and natural law represent attempts to apply
moral principles to political relationships. They have a
long and complicated history. But consent theory is a
relatively new justification for political authority. The
notion that political authority rests upon some identifiable
and voluntary act of the citizenry emerged from the
political conflicts of the seventeenth and eighteenth centuries. Consent theory became increasingly connected with
liberalism and later, with democratic government.
Moreover, its premises were more than congenial to a

world which viewed man as autonomous and rational and politics as conventional and artificial.

The doctrine of consent is now firmly imbedded in our vocabulary of politics. It is difficult for us to imagine a government deserving obedience which does not rest upon consent. Robert Dahl conveys conventional political wisdom when he says: "Government without one's consent can be an affront to human dignity and respect. We see this most vividly in extreme cases — the hapless victim in a concentration camp, who is subjected to the utmost humiliation, degradation, depravation, and torture, loses thereby a part of his humanity."[1] Yet despite their unchallenged position (or perhaps because of it) consent theorists have yet to present us with a clear analysis of political obligation. They have insisted that the basis of obedience to the state rests with consent but they have been far from clear in telling us precisely what consent is, how it creates moral duty, and how consent to a government creates a moral obligation to obey that government. John Plamenatz has remarked that John Locke, the most famous of the consent theorists, begins with a concept of consent too rigorous to allow for any legitimate government and ends with a notion so loose that any government would be justified simply by having power to put down attempts at rebellion. In fact, this paper will contend that all consent theories exhibit this curious elasticity. They veer alternately, often in the same work, toward both a justification of anarchy and of absolutism. The broader purpose of this chapter then will be to do for consent theorists what they have failed to do for themselves — to determine what we mean when we say "I consent," to analyze what we might call the "structural apparatus of consent" (how consent obliges, how far it obliges, and why it obliges) , and to examine how we might determine what "counts" as consent to a government and how far that consent obliges one to obey a government.

Consent theorists are not a homogeneous lot. They offer readers numerous interpretations of what consent is, how it works, and how far it obliges. Such disagreement would not be an insuperable problem if we were able to find a consistent and clear line of development within any particular consent theory. Unfortunately, this is a benefit we are rarely permitted to enjoy. Yet, it may be possible to outline various positions on consent and its relation to moral duty and political obligation. We will find that some consent theorists hold to more than one position despite the fact that the views on consent in each may well be mutually exclusive.

Consent as approval: strong and weak versions

This position sees consent as an expression of approval or recognition. There is some disagreement, however, over what should be taken as constituting recognition or approval. A strong version of this theory contends that approval is dependent either upon the existence of certain political institutions or, at least, upon individual judgments about the direction of government.

This is clearly the position taken by Hannah Pitkin in her recent attempt to relate anew consent and political obligation.[2] She contends that to consent is to "recognize [government] as an authority" but that traditional consent theory is defective: "It directs a man's attention to the wrong place. It teaches him to look at himself (for his own consent) or at the people around him (for theirs), rather than at the merits of the government."[3] Her doctrine, which she calls "hypothetical consent," contends that obligation depends not on whether you have consented but on whether the government is such that you ought to consent to it:

> Your obligation depends not on any actual act of consenting, past or present, by yourself or your fellow citizens, but on the character of your government. If it is a good, just government doing what a government should, then you must obey it, if it is a tyrannical unjust government trying to do what no government may, then you have no such obligation.[4]

The second and weaker version of this position contains a much broader conception of approval in that acquiescence is regarded as evidence of consent. John Locke employs this version in at least two instances in his *Second Treatise*. First, he uses this position to justify inequality in property ownership:

> But since gold and silver, being little useful to the Life of Man in proportion to Food, Rayment and Carriage, has its value only from the consent of men, whereof Labour yet makes, in great part, the measure, it is plain, that Men have agreed to disproportionate and unequal possession of the Earth, they having by a tacit and voluntary consent found out a way, how a man may fairly possess more land that he himself can use the product of, by receiving in exchange for the overplus, gold and silver.[5]

Yet one is not in a position to ask "When did I consent?" to a coin exchange. Locke merely tells us that "Fancy or Agreement" led men to place value upon them.[6] Men simply do recognize money as exchange and Locke is willing to count this recognition as consent. Lest one fail to see the significance of the consequences of this application of consent, let him note Locke's position on labor relations. While Locke insists that a master may not take away a servant's life or "at pleasure, so much as maim him but the loss of an Eye or Tooth," a contract of "Drudgery" is clearly obligatory as is "the Subjection of the Needy Beggar . . . who preferred being his [Master's] subject to starving."7

Locke's use of consent to justify political authority is well known: "No one can be . . . subjected to the Political Power of another without his own consent." Yet when Locke asks, "What shall be understood to be a sufficient Declaration of a Man's Consent, to make him subject to the laws of any government?"8 He arrives at two distinct positions on consent. For those who "by actual Agreement, and . . . express Declaration" give their consent, Locke outlines a theory of consent which will be discussed in a moment. For those who have made "no Expressions of it at all," Locke offers a theory of tacit consent. One has consented (and is thereby obligated) if he owns property or even is "largely travelling freely on the Highway."9 Locke even admits that tacit consent "reaches as far as the very being of any one within the Territories of that Government."10

Now this does indeed appear to be a strange doctrine. It asserts, in effect, that one is obligated because he consented or because, even though he didn't actually consent, he is obligated because he exists. This seems a far cry from the stringent individualism with which Locke is associated. What, after all, does it mean to say that consent must be individually given and then to say that the mere occupation of space counts as consent? Thus John Plamenatz in his classic work on consent irately concludes that "to live under the protection of a certain government does not constitute consent to the existence of that government. . . . It does not impose upon the protected person an obligation to obey them [laws]."11 The point, however, is this: precisely how does Locke's concept of tacit consent attempt to answer the question "Why should I obey the state?" Plamenatz is quite right in saying that living under the protection of a certain government does not constitute consent to the existence of that government nor an obligation to it. Living within a state does not presuppose the recognition of obligation to that government. It does, however, still permit one to ask the question "Why obey the law?" and possibly respond by saying that in lieu of continuing to enjoy certain privileges I will consent to obey what it commands. But it can easily work the other way also. Enjoying an estate and enjoying the use of a highway or even enjoying fresh air are very different privileges. The person benefiting from the latter may well see fit to answer that the continuation of breathing fresh air within a given territory is simply not worth consenting to this law. In any case, before this question is asked, and indeed answered in a certain way, consent has not been given. Ironically Locke's error lay in failing to distinguish the act of consent from the reasons which might move one to consent. The latter (what Locke called tacit consent) is not consent at all, but only a preliminary consideration to the question "Why should I obey the law?" Locke clearly jumped the gun. He loaded the question by placing it within the consent apparatus.[12]

There are others, however, both within and outside academic circles who appear to accept this Lockean position without reservation.[13] I should like to speak of only one particular writer in this context — Joseph Tussman in his *Obligation and the Body Politic*.[14] Tussman's book is ideal for our purpose since it sets out to advance systematically this position where others only treat it with a passing reference.

Tussman begins with much the same purpose in mind as we have suggested. If we are to be able to account for political obligation in moral terms, then, given the fact that the notion of the state deprives each of us of a right to a whole range of actions, we must offer an account that sees the individual's relation to the state as voluntary. This is Tussman's point as well. The "body politic" may be seen in a variety of ways: (1) as a membership subordinate to a single coercive power; (2) as a membership sharing in a common set of habits; (3) as a membership party to a system of agreements on the model of a voluntary association.[15] Only in the last case can we speak of a relationship in which "I have a moral obligation" can apply. Tussman proceeds to ask a crucial question: "Are we satisfied with the answer that accepting this subordination (or private judgment to public judgment) is what 'being moral' or 'being a good citizen' really means?"[16] The answer, for Tussman at least, lies in terms of a series of decidedly naturalistic justifications. The voluntary character of membership in a body politic involves: " (1) Some justifications for the subordination in the light of the interests and purposes of the individual. (2) Recognition of some common or shared concern. (3) Some recognition that one's own interests constitute only a subordinate part of a broader system of interests."[17]

Thus far our summary of Tussman's position does not sound terribly unlike the "strong" interpretation of consent which we noted earlier. Consent is conceived as recognition, and recognition varies from approval of the character of a particular government to approval of the need for government. In fact, the above description of the "body politic" could be readily acceptable to a philosophical anarchist. But it is at this point that Tussman's position begins to show itself as a very loose conception of consent indeed and in addition (and more importantly for our purposes) begins to show how elusive is the concept of consent itself. The nature of obligation to the state is compared to the decision-making apparatus of a caucus:

> It is generally assumed or expected that the caucus decision will not be unanimous; for if unanimity is required the caucus agreement is pointless. It is precisely the failure of unanimity which makes the caucus necessary. There is thus both a presupposition of unanimity and a deliberate repetition of the demand for unanimity. The sense in which unanimity is presupposed is the sense in which everyone who is a member is a party to the agreement. But the unanimous agreement is to the bindingness of subsequent non-unanimous decisions and, in this form, to the subordination of individual judgment to group judgment and decision.[18]

Tussman concludes that "considering this it is hardly surprising that the agreement to waive unanimity should come to be regarded as *the* social compact."[19] These statements are indeed the core of all traditional consent theory, and we should not be surprised if it is at this point that the theory begins to lose plausibility.

Since Tussman is attempting to use consent as a vehicle for a theory of moral obligation to the state, he must convince us that the decision to agree unanimously to future nonunanimous decision-making is voluntary. But he then places himself in the position of having to contend that such a set of decisions actually do or did take place. It will not do for him to say that there are such things as moral obligations to the state and that they are derived from individual voluntary acts of recognition or agreement with the state but that these acts in fact never really took place. We simply cannot say that they could or can take place because until they have there is no consent and thus, on these terms, no moral obligation. Hypothetical reasoning, although it has many valid uses in terms of other moral concepts, cannot be used as a basis for *establishing* consent. While it is true that we can say that there can be no moral obligations to the state until one consents, we must reserve our evaluation of whether such obligations exist until we actually decide if anyone has consented. To say that in any political system people should or would consent and thus have a moral obligation to the state is really to base moral obligation to the state upon an apparatus other than consent simply because consent (by one's own admission) has not been given.

It is now easy to see why Pitkin's reformulation of consent is really no longer consent at all. To say that if a government is good then you must obey it is completely irrelevant to consent.[20] Tussman, however, does not give up so easily. He sets out to do what consent theory has always said it could do — establish how the body politic actually does consent. Once we see how this is done we shall find that consent, even on Tussman's own terms, becomes irrelevant to obligation, though in a way very different from Pitkin's concept.

Right on cue, Tussman notes "the assertion that the citizen of a body politic is a party to a system of agreements inevitably evokes the surprised response — 'when did I agree to any such thing?'"[21] Like so many consent theorists Tussman notes instances which indicate that consent has taken place: the creation of a new body politic by explicit agreement (the promulgation and ratification of the U.S. Constitution, the creation of the United Nations) and the naturalization of citizens. But then comes the rub. Tussman admits, "We fall back . . . upon the familiar notion of tacit consent." The difference between tacit and express consent is not the difference beetwen two kinds of consent. It is only the difference in the way consent is given:

Not only may there be other verbal acts which can be interpreted as the giving of consent, but there may be non-verbal acts which have the same force. So that the question of tacit consent is the question of whether there are some actions, including perhaps, the failure to act, which can properly be regarded as the equivalent of the express consent given by the naturalized citizen.[22]

Yet Tussman hesitates at a most crucial juncture. He refuses to tell us what acts may be taken as tacit consent: "It is not profitable . . . to argue abstractly about the acts which can be taken as a sign that one has become a party to the system of agreements constituting a body politic."[23] The only condition for tacit consent that he will offer us is that it must be given "knowingly." Consent and subsequent obligation do not revolve about particular institutions or practices and one's participation in them. Saluting the flag, registering for conscription, voting, filing one's income for taxes, or even using a zip code on mail could all be taken as instances of consent if the citizen by performing these acts understands that he has incurred obligations to the state. Consent, then, is a radically individual personal action. One could do all the above things and simply not conceive of them as consent. But even here a note of skepticism seeps in: "But we must accept it as a plain fact that many native 'citizens' have in no meaningful sense agreed to anything. They have never been asked and have never thought about it. They are political childbrides who have a status they do not understand and which they have not acquired by their own consent."[24] There is by Tussman's own admission a "shrinkage" in the body politic. The solution Tussman offers to this "shrinkage" is the only one available to him if he wishes to retain consent as a basis of moral obligation to the state. But it is also one which on examination ultimately wreaks havoc with the concept of consent: "Non-consenting adult citizens are, in effect, like minors who are governed without their own consent. The period of tutelage and dependence is unduly prolonged."25 Tussman's theory is complete. When is one obligated to obey and when not? One is obligated when he consents, tacitly or expressly. If one does not give his consent he is obligated as a child. Whom is one obligated to obey? He is obligated to obey the legitimate authority presiding over the body politic. The legitimate authority is that government to which one has consented or refused to consent. The paradox is painfully clear. One either consents, of if he fails to consent, is placed under a moral tutelage until he does — in which case the absence of consent "as a failure of political education" exists in any political system. Or consent is somehow unrelated to obligations to the state since one is obligated whether he consents or does not.

Part of both Tussman's and Pitkin's problems with offering a viable account of consent lies in their failure to evaluate systematically the whole apparatus of consent, i.e., to ask what really does it mean to consent? We shall ask this question for ourselves shortly. But another part of their problem lies in choosing an inappropriate definition of consent. Our next task then is to look at two positions which see consent not as approval or recognition but as a far different sort of operation.

Consent as permission, 1

We are now about to begin upon a road toward the reconstruction of the concept of consent and again we will find, ironically, that John Locke can lead the way for us. The reader will recall that according to Locke, men in the state of nature, are in a "state of perfect

Freedom to order their Actions, and dispose of their Possessions and Persons as they think fit, within the bounds of the Law of Nature, without asking leave, or depending upon the Will of any other Man."[26] The only way this condition can be altered is through the act of consent:

> Men being, as has been said by Nature, all free, equal and independent, no one can be put out of his Estate, and subjected to the Political Power of another, without his own Consent. The only way whereby anyone divests himself of his Natural Liberty, and puts on the bounds of Civil Society is by agreeing with other Men to join and unite into a Community.[27]

Men born under existing government become obliged only when by some explicit act they give permission to a government: "And thus the Consent of Free-men, born under Government, which only makes them Members of it, being given separately in their turns, as each comes to be of Age, and not in a multitude together."[28] Merely living under the jurisdiction of government may oblige one to the extent that one recognizes that others (by Locke's definition, members of civil society) have consented to it but that such an obligation to submit to the government "begins and ends with the Enjoyment."[29] Nothing can make a man a subject or member of civil society save "his actually entering into it by positive Engagement, and express Promise and Compact."[30]

In the position on consent which we had previously stated, we indicated that in its strong version, consent was interpreted so exactingly that not only could no government live up to it but that the concept really involved no "consenting" at all. The weak version erred on the opposite side. It became impossible to envisage any subject-ruler relationship that could not be interpreted as being based upon consent. This part of Locke's formulation appears to avoid both these pitfalls. It does so, I think, because it incorporates certain basic features which the previous theories failed to realize. First Locke, at least in this instance, does not treat the act of consent as an act of approval or as an act of recognition or agreement. Consent becomes an act of permission. We can safely call it such because Locke tells us that there are certain actions which the state may now undertake, especially in terms of the regulation of property, which it could not have previously legitimately undertaken. I may approve of state actions but the right of the state to pursue certain objectives as they relate to me is irrelevant to my approval. I may, by action or word, recognize the existence of the state, but that recognition is independent of an act of permission. This is a very important distinction, and Locke's concepts of express and tacit consent and his insistence that they oblige differently account for this (albeit, in a very oblique way).

The distinction between approval or recognition is so crucial to the concept of consent and to political theory in general that is is necessary at this point to expend some effort at clarification. Let me begin by using a very simple illustration. A friend takes my television set without my knowledge. Missing the set, I call him and ask him if he knows where it is. He tells me that he took it to repair it and, in fact, that now it is in perfect working order. Faced with my consternation, he may ask, "Didn't you want the set repaired? Aren't you glad it's fixed? Why are you so upset?" My reply might be that my pleasure with the set is not the point. The point is that no one had the right to take the set without my permission. Now we may contend that I am being unduly harsh with my friend. After all, his intentions were admirable, he is competent, and he does live just around the block. The intentions of the state, however, are not always as easily discernible, nor is its competency, nor are the individuals' powers of retrieval as proximate. But we are getting a bit ahead of ourselves. We shall return to this question shortly.

Consent conceived as permission contains the same radical individualism as the weak version of the approval theory. The difference is that the language of permission forces us to consider the precise role that consent plays in terms of a transfer of moral rights. Heretofore the legitimacy of an action was related to my recognition of the rightness of the action or to my approval of its effects. Traditional consent theory then proceeds to limit this operation by placing consent in a particular time sequence in relation to the acts in question. One may explicitly recognize or approve of an action in time period T_1 and find that this recognition or approval binds him in T_2 for the same or even new actions. For example, Smith takes Jones's television set in order to repair it. Jones, even though he had no knowledge of Smith's action, recognizes and approves of it by accepting the set and saying "thank you." Did Jones's recognition and approval bind him to loan his television set to Smith at any future time? Did it bind him to accept the television set if the second time it was returned it was damaged? How far, in short, does Jones's consent (as approval or recognition) to the first action bind him to submit to other actions (similar or dissimilar) in the future? Is Jones now bound to accept Smith's appropriation, temporary or permanent, of his dishwasher or his books or even his children? At this point the reader might object. Surely Jones's original action bound him only to accept that particular set at that particular time or at most bound him to accept all of Smith's actions designed to meet Jones's wishes. Any more inclusive interpretations of Jones's consent, the reader might conclude, sounds ridiculous. Yet there are clear and substantial reasons why the larger interpretations of Jones's consent do indeed sound ridiculous. These reasons can be contained within a theory of consent. Yet they become muddled in traditional consent theory. How much different is it to say that men, by living in a particular society, thereby consent to that society's medium of economic exchange, or to say that men by agreeing to be bound to the decisions of a caucus are henceforth bound to subsequent decisions of that body, or to say that in voting one is thereby bound to accept the commands of the winner than it is to say that Jones by consenting to Smith's appropriation of his television set is bound to accept Smith's appropriation of his wife?

The reason the approval theory of consent fails to account for these questions is that its approach does not lead one to consider the relation between the act of consent and moral duty. Our discussion indicated two crucial questions about consent and moral duty: How far (both in terms of time and scope of action) does consent bind? Does consent rise from a nexus between an expression of desire or a wish and its fulfillment on the part of another? Traditional consent theory always answers yes to the second question and then always denies the relation between wish and fulfillment in later actions. Consent is born from a favorable conjunction of approval and fulfillment, but like a Frankenstein, it lives on long after that conjunction has dissipated. The reader will remember that we said that the consent apparatus is a structure which enables obligations to occur within the context of the suspension of moral judgment. Therefore, within the confines of a consent apparatus it is not a genuine argument to contend that "because you agreed" as an answer to the question "Why am I obligated?" is misplaced and should rather be "because it is right." The whole purpose of the consent apparatus is to shift the answer to "Why am I obligated?" away from considerations of moral judgment. The failure of the approval theory of consent, however, is that it is unable to account for a plausible relationship with moral duty.

Both the approval and permission theories of consent focus upon the features and circumstances surrounding the original actions of the parties. In approval theory one asks did I "agree or approve" of the action in question in order to find what is a morally correct course of action. The permission theory asks did I give "permission" to the action in question. The difference is crucial to a plausible account of consent. In the former case, one's duty is determined by his actions or words in relation to another party. He either agreed to Smith's actions, wished Smith would have done a particular action, or approved of Smith's action. These attitudes indicate how far he is bound to Smith's action. Nothing is said about how consent obliges apart from the notion that the conjunction between agreement, approval, or wish and its fulfillment obliges. It sounds nonsensical for me to say that I have consented to my neighbor's mowing of his lawn because I agree or approve or wish that he would do so. Yet many accept without so much as a blink of an eyelash the assertion that because I approve of the president's policies or wish he would make a decision on an issue which he later does, I have consented to the policies or to the president or to both. I have approved of the policies but nowhere have I consented to them. The point that we are making is this: the approval theory of consent fails to make clear that the act of consent involves the transfer or creation of moral rights which could not otherwise exist. John Plamenatz has stated this position very succinctly: "The giving of consent is essentially the granting of permission, and there cannot be action by permission unless the right of the agent to act depends for its existence upon the granting of permission."[31] There are then all sorts of actions one might agree to. One may agree to have his daughter marry. Yet we cannot call this an act of consent until we are in a position to say that one's daughter could not, morally speaking, marry *without* her father's permission. The approval theory so neglects this aspect of consent that its pronouncements, at least in terms of political theory, often produce a "what's yours is mine and what's mine is mine" account of obligation.

There are a number of other features of the consent apparatus which must be discussed before we can safely say that we have provided an account of consent, but the permission theory, as indicated by Locke and as so clearly stated by Plamenatz, gives us our foundation. A theory of consent must apply to situations in which permission is necessary before an agent has the right to perform the action in question.

In summary then, the position regarding consent which we have just outlined is superior to both versions of the approval theory in that it emphasizes the significance of the act of consent in relation to the performance of specific actions. It does this by using language which emphasizes the enlargement of moral authority which takes place in a consenting act and by clarifying where moral rights lie before and after the act of consent. This interpretation of consent is particularly constraining when it is applied to political affairs, and it should not surprise us to learn that few liberal democratic theorists have been willing to accept it. For it contends in effect that consent fails to provide for an adequate account of political obligation unless those holding office are unable to perform any action without the permission of the citizenry. Since even the most democratic political systems operate without this necessary qualification and only act as if they had met this prerequisiste, one must reach the position that the rights of the governors exist independent of the consent of the governed or that the governors indeed have no rights at all. It is interesting to note that Locke, while using this notion of consent, never indicated how many of the governed had indeed expressly consented to the state and only assumed that they had when he later spoke of the justifications for revolt. John Plamenatz appears to be the only writer to have held this position and seen it to its logical conclusion:

We see then, that both under pure democracy and under representative democracy there is no such thing as government by the consent of all persons supposed to owe obedience to government. Under the very best possible conditions, so far as consent is concerned, it may be true that the rights of the governors depend upon the consent of a majority of governed, but never upon the consent of all persons who can rightly be said to be obliged to obey the law.[32]

Consent as permission, 2

There is, however, a third position on consent, one which continues to conceive of consent as permission but also is willing to count participation in, or the existence of, certain political practices as evidence of permission.[33] Here is a position which is so widely accepted in modern democratic theory that no one takes the trouble to attempt to justify it. One writer who has taken the trouble is, paradoxically, John Plamenatz. Plamenatz in *Man and Society* and in his postscript to the second edition of *Consent, Freedom and Political Obligation* now admits that his "definition [of consent] was too narrow," that "where there is an established process of election to an office, then . . . anyone who takes part in the process consents to the authority of whoever is elected to the office."[34] His larger argument is contained below:

When you vote for a person or party that wins an election you directly consent to his or their authority, and you also consent indirectly to the system of government. Even when your vote is cast for persons who intend to change the system you consent until it is changed. For you make use of the system in order to change it. . . . Even if you dislike the system and wish to change it, you put yourself by your vote under an obligation to obey whatever government comes legally to power under the system, and this can properly be called giving consent. For the purpose of an election is to give authority to the people who win it, and if you vote knowing what you are doing and without being compelled to do it, you voluntarily take part in the process which gives authority to those people. It does not matter what your motive is, any more than it matters what your motive is in making a promise.[35]

Plamenatz defends his correlation of voting with consent as one which makes "ordinary use of one of the most important terms in the political vocabulary."[36] Indeed, one of the most important points lost in this position is that consent belongs to a moral vocabulary and not a political one. But the reader has waited long enough for a systematic analysis of consent. The election position finally forces us to undertake such an analysis. For in order to judge whether voting establishes obligation via consent, we must ask how consent is precisely related to obligation. And since when one votes he is not consenting as such but in Plamenatz's words "can be said to consent," we must ask precisely what consent is with a view toward deciding how close voting is indeed to consenting.

We have already seen that a good deal of the confusion over consent theories of political obligation has been related to an inadequate examination of what consent really is. We will attempt to remedy this condition by analyzing what we might call the structural apparatus of consent. Statements in political thought such as "governments derive their just powers from the consent of the governed" or "political parties are the vehicles for consent in modern democracies" and phrases such as "express and tacit" consent and "direct and indirect" consent all depend upon a conception of the operation of consent for their intelligibility. Before, however, we are in a position to decide what counts as consent, if indeed anything can, we must discover both what it means to say "I consent" and what one actually *does* when he consents.

Consent has a number of features common to other sorts of apparatus which give rise to obligations. When one consents, as when one promises or contracts, he is engaged in some commitment to do, or forbear from, some future action. One simply cannot say "I promise to quit smoking last year" or "I contract with Jones to build a dam last month" just as one cannot say "I consent to your marriage last week." The past tenses of "promise," "contract," or "consent" are used solely to explain or justify one's present obligations. To say "you promised" or "you consented" is a way of saying your time is up; the pay-off is the performance of an obligation incurred in a previous time period. Promising, consenting, and contracting are future-oriented acts when they take place. It is the obligations they incur which are explained in terms of past actions. Consenting also is a relational term. One consents to someone else, just as one promises someone else or contracts with someone else. While we do have a grammar which allows for an internal dialogue using these terms, such as "I promise myself" or "I have permitted myself (a piece of cake) ," it is not altogether clear that it has any significance for moral philosophy.

Unlike contracting, however, consent, in terms of the obligations incurred, does not involve reciprocal relationships. If the reader will recall social contract theory, he will note that for Hobbes the agreement between "every man with every man" involves obligations on the part of all parties: "I Authorize and give up my Right of Governing myself, to this Man, or to this Assembly of men, on this condition, that thou give up thy Right to him, and Authorize all his in like manner."[37] When an agent consents, however, he limits his actions while the recipient actually has his enlarged. When a father, for instance, consents to the marriage of his daughter, he incurs certain obligations. He not only must refrain from disrupting the ceremony, he must refrain from ordering his daughter about henceforth. The prospective husband, on the other hand, incurs no obligations, at least in terms of consent. On the contrary, he now has the *right* to perform actions otherwise unavailable to him. If I consentt o have my television fixed, I incur obligations which arise from its repair. These may even include an obligation to pay for repairs I had no anticipated. The repairman, on the other hand, now has a right to repair my set. Again, he incurs no obligations toward me as a recipient of my consent. The point of all this is simply that both parties in a consenting act assume new moral roles. The agent is placed in a passive and obligatory role, while the recipient takes on an active (in the sense that the future action in question is his to "do") and claimant role.[38]

The consenting act then is a nonreciprocal one. The agent does not get something in return by consenting. Although he may have reciprocity in mind when he consents, the consenting act itself makes no demands in terms of mutual performance of action. It is certainly possible for one to say that he will consent to X if the recipient consents to do Y. But then we have two consenting acts being proposed here. This relationship is quite different from a contractual arrangement in that mutual obligation is part of the act in question. The contract's relation to moral duty, of course, need not necessarily prove to be any more clear-cut. One may have second thoughts about the moral correctness of the contract or he may find that the performance of the obligation of a contract violates obligations he has subsequently incurred toward others. Nevertheless, when one consents, the demand for reciprocity as a payment for obligations is not a relevant argument.

The unique structural features of consent, its nonreciprocity, the unequal demands placed upon consenting parties, and the incurring of obligations to action in the future, may damage its connection with moral duty when applied to the affairs of state. That is to say, these features of consent when applied to a context in which the agent is the citizen and the recipient the state may drastically accentuate the inequality of services and obligations which are already part of its structure. While consent theory has the merit of indicating that a government must somehow depend upon the governed for one to speak of obligations, the very apparatus which is employed to convey this position may work in the other direction. When one gives his consent to another person, we have seen that he has constricted his own moral autonomy. He has, in fact, transferred that autonomy to the recipient of his consent. When that recipient is the state, the individual's ability to retrieve or define his consent is limited in a way uncommon to personal relationships. The limitation is not merely the result of an existing system of legal sanctions in the hands of one of the parties to the consenting act. It is also limited by the resources available to the state as it defines its role as recipient of an obligation. Officials of the state are in a position to speak over the head of the agent to the whole citizenry. A citizenry cannot be expected to accept readily the claims of an individual agent under the conditions of such an unequal forum. Should an agent ally himself with other like-minded agents to press their case, the state again is in a position to define what it considers the group claims to be. These are rarely placed in a favorable light. The point we must remember is that when the agent of consent, either an individual or a group, claims that permission was not granted on a policy of the government, the position of the state is such that it can effectively appeal to the rest of the citizenry by defining the contest of claims in its own terms. When the government speaks, its voice is heard by more people and with more plausibility.

This presents a significant problem in the application of the doctrine of consent to political theory. Democratic theory, in particular, attempts to save the doctrine by emphasizing the role of elections and the right to organize opposition. The election certainly may make the agent's task of withdrawing consent easier. Most of us would agree that the job of electing another person or party to office is a bit easier than engaging in successful revolution. Nevertheless, if elections are to be justified as a practice which affords the agent an opportunity to withdraw his consent from a government, the very participation in an election cannot also be made to count as consent. That is, the fact that a political system affords its citizens the opportunity to change a government and/or its policies does not necessarily mean that system is based upon consent. It may be true that free elections are necessary for one to be able to speak of government by consent in the sense that elections hold out the possibility for the agent to contest openly the claims of the state as recipient. But then the practice of elections in itself is not an act of consent. If it were, a citizen could not withdraw permission except by not voting. If he participates in the election process at all he is consenting. The practice of elections then does not contain the option of withdrawing consent. This interpretation shows its basic absurdity if we ask What can a citizen do if he wishes to withhold or withdraw his consent to the government? He cannot vote for any opposition because the act of voting commits him to consent to the winner. Now if the incumbent's chances of sucess are greater than the insurgent's and if the citizen refuses to give consent to the incumbent, our advice to him is not to vote at all. This strategy hardly affords a justification of elections for democracies. The more intense the opposition to the incumbent, the more likely are the chances of an incumbent victory. Any voter who may feel intensely about the current government had best not vote at all. Voting is only an activity to be undertaken when one is quite willing to see either party win or only has a slight preference for one over the other. In that case, elections remain a basis for consent but they hardly provide the role for which they are intended. They can no longer be a vehicle of change or opposition. Ironically, we find that if we insist that voting is consent, then opposition to a government becomes fundamentally the same sort of opposition that a citizen must undertake in an authoritarian state, extralegal action. Our only other alternative is to contend that elections are relevant to consent in the sense that they provide the equivalent in politics of what we would call rational argument in moral disputes. That is, the election is a way in which the citizen as agent can "talk" to the government as recipient. But the consenting act itself must have occurred outside the structure of elections. Clearly voting is not the same as talking in many respects, the most significant of which is that in voting one has actually made a decision rather than merely talked about it. But then the fact that we allow the citizen to say only "no" or "yes" to the state is the price we must pay if we choose to rest political obligation upon consent.

We have yet one more question to answer, however, before we can ask if the price we must pay for consent is indeed too high. What precisely is the relationship between consent and moral duty? How far does consent oblige? We have just completed an examination of the structure of the consenting act. What we are about to do now is ask how far consent goes toward explaining one's moral duty. They are, I think, three important requirements that must be met for consent to give rise to obligation on the part of both the agent and recipient:

1. The recipient must receive some right which he would not be morally justified in asserting without the consent of the agent.

2. An agent must have existing moral authority over

an object to give his consent to some use of it. One cannot consent to have another's property sold simply because it is not his.

3. Consent does not mean that standards of rightness become irrelevant to doing one's duty. The agent in a consenting act is not limited to consideration of whether he gave permission to the act in question. Although consent is an apparatus designed to eliminate contingency between moral agents, it may sometimes be necessary for an agent to ask questions other than "did I consent?" in determining duty. Returning a gun to a man whom one has learned is a psychopath is not doing one's duty.

The reader can see that consent gives rise to moral duty only under certain circumstances: when an agent possesses moral rights, when a recipient can acquire those rights only by permission, and when obligations assumed take place within the boundaries of moral rightness. Consent is irrelevant to moral duty when an agent has an obligation to perform an act simply because he (morally) ought to do so. Only certain classes of actions require permission to make them (morally) right for the recipient to do. Democratic theory has assumed the burden of contending that all obligations of the citizenry and all rights of the government are the result of consenting acts.[39] Nevertheless, it remains clear that consent explains moral duty only under certain circumstances. One can indeed ask, "Why should I consent to X, when I am already obliged because to do X is right?" Consent is even more circumscribed when we consider that granting permission cannot be the final answer in the determination of moral duty. When Locke contended that men could not give their consent to slavery, he was saying that giving permission cannot explain certain obligations. When one asserts that voting is consent he fails to take into account the objects of consent. Consent indeed is a procedure. But it is a procedure which gives rise to substantive obligations. The question "Was I right to consent?" is a secondary question but it is a question which may need to be answered nonetheless. When it is, one must ask "What did I consent to?" with a view toward assessing the obligations he has incurred. If I have no obligation to respect my daughter's marriage to a psychopath even though I consented, then I have no obligation to obey a prime minister who makes a set of morally disastrous decisions even though I voted for him. Refusing to perform obligations incurred by consent is a solemn act but it may certainly be consistent with doing one's duty.

No other modern political theory can compete with liberalism in its dedication and relative success in demythologizing politics. What so angered Hobbes's contemporaries was not his authoritarianism but the forthrightness with which he justified it. Even the current criticism of American pluralism, the most timid of liberal theories of politics, has focused upon its realism and alleged cynicism regarding political power.[40] Universally accepted political shibboleths have crumbled against liberal onslaughts. Divine sanction, class virtue, custom, even majority rule have been subjected to the srutiny of liberals. The notion that the state is to be evaluated solely on the basis of its performance in meeting basic, if prosaic, needs is a concept that is historically new in political thought and not even universally accepted today.

Not the least of the virtues of liberalism has been its refusal to introduce a political mythology of its own. Yet the doctrine of consent is an exception; it is liberalism's retreat to the figurative in politics. Rarely does a liberal insist on the "reality" of an admitted fiction except with the adoption of consent theory. In all fairness, it should be noted that the temptations of consent theory are very great. The doctrine of consent treats political action as an act of volition and as such resolves the liberal dilemma of accounting for political authority. Moreover, consent theory, especially in its archetypal form of the social contract, conceives of politics in a manner congenial to the liberal mind. A short digression can illustrate. Jean Piaget has contended that the development of morality in the child from a very crude heteronomy in the form of commands of a parent to autonomy is achieved through an intermediary stage of reciprocity.[41] The child views the morality of an action in terms of its conformity with contracts and promises. Piaget observed that at this stage the insistence upon the observance of contracts is to the adult's eyes ruthless and uncompromising. The child will accept no excuse, no extenuating circumstance as a justification for non-performance. The Swiss psychologist tells us that this stage is essential to the development of a capacity for individual moral judgment with all the uncertainties and strains that its decisions involve. For the liberal, political authorities can never reach a stage of full moral adulthood. So affected by the flow of power available to them, governmental officials need to be restrained by a sense of contractual morality. One can expect no more from those in political organization. Yet the irony of this whole approach is that not only does the liberal foster a restricted view of the possibilities of moral judgment on the part of the governed but he finds that he himself, as one who is governed, must submit to a truncated ethics as well. The first protest or the first questioning of a decision is followed by a command to silence as ruthless and demanding as that of the ten year old, "But you consented!"

It is difficult to admit but, as we shall indicate in more detail in chapter 5, the acceptance of a differential moral rationality between rulers and ruled is as much a result of consent theory as an uneven application of it. Two hundred years ago Bentham, in his attack on the consent theory of Sir William Blackstone, told his readers that the "season of fiction is now over." Let us admit that while it will always be relevant to ask "What right have you to do X, as I never consented?", the particular relationship between consent and moral duty, the inability to find practices which can sensibly "count" as consent in political systems, and the very structure of consent itself makes it a very unlikely basis for an answer to "Why should I obey the state?"

4

Slippage:
The Odd Debt of Gratitude

> They say over here you are choking
> to death on your cities and slaves,
> but they have never smelled dry grass
> smoked Kools in a drugstore,
> or pronounced a flat "a," an honest "r."
> Don't read your reviews,
> A * M * E * R * I * C * A
> You are the only land—*John Updike*

> The state ought not to be considered as nothing better
> than a partnership agreement in a trade of pepper or
> coffee, calico, or tobacco, or some other such low concern.
> . . . It is to be looked on with other reverence.
>
> —*Edmund Burke*

THE LIBERAL belief in the desirability of eliminating emotions (even moral ones) from politics and confining any poetic sense of community to social and individual efforts has not been easy to live up to. The emotive impulse has nearly always crept into the liberal polity. It has done so through a natural and seemingly innocent concept: the commonly recognized duty of gratitude. Moreover, because of the accounts of political obligation available to liberal political thought, the duty of gratitude itself has been introduced surreptitiously. We will begin to illustrate this contention by examining the positions of three very different political philosophers (including the argument of one who historically has stood for the antithesis of liberal politics) who employ what ostensibly looks like a contract/consent model of political obligation but which on examination becomes indistinguishable from a gratitude model of political obligation. Secondly, we will examine the gratitude model in the full light of day and suggest its significance in liberal political thought.

Plato, Hobbes, Locke: the suppressed gratitude model

Plato considers the relationship between citizen and state most succinctly and dramatically in the *Crito*. Socrates, charged and convicted of impiety and corruption of youth, denies both allegations and declares that he never intentionally wronged anyone. Crito visits Socrates in prison, offers to help him escape, and is puzzled by his friend's refusal. Socrates replies, first by quickly convincing Crito that "neither injury nor retaliation nor warding off evil by evil is ever right" and then by imaging what the voice of the laws would say to the would-be fugitive:

Consider, Socrates, if we are speaking truly that in your present attempt you are doing to do us an injury. For, having brought you into the world, and nurtured and educated you, and given you and every other citizen a share in every good which we had to give, we further proclaim to any Athenian by the liberty which we allow him, that if he does not like us when he has become of age and has seen the ways of the city, and made our acquaintance, he may go where he pleases and take his goods with him. None of us laws forbid him or interfere with him. Any one who does not like us and the city, and who wants to emigrate to a colony or to any other city, may go where he likes, returning his property. But he who has experience of the manner in which we order justice and administer the State, and still remains, has entered into an implied contract that he will do as we command him.[1]

Since the laws remind Socrates that he had seventy years to reflect on the terms of the covenant and never left Athens ("the halt, the blind, the maimed were not more stationary in her than you were"[2]), they conclude that in fleeing he would be doing "what only a miserable slave would do, running away and turning your back upon the compacts and agreements which you made as a citizen."[3] Crito is unable to respond to this appeal, and Socrates soon drinks the hemlock.

Plato's argument is really a very simple one:

1. Contracts are obligatory.
2. Residence is equivalent to a contract.
3. Socrates is a resident.
4. Socrates is obliged to obey.

In fact, Plato has given such significance to the contract as a justification for obedience that it appears that, by definition, the decision of the state, despite Socrates' admonitions in the *Apology,* is just. It is with the laws that Socrates has contracted. While it is true that certain men in authority have been unjust to Socrates they are not parties to the contract. Since Plato would have us believe that Socrates cannot disobey the interpretors of the laws without flaunting the laws themselves, justice demands that Socrates accept his sentence.

Yet the argument that permits Plato to refuse to allow one to disobey a law while remaining loyal to the state gains its plausibility only because it contains a second (and hidden) argument. Intermingled with the previous argument for a contract analogy is an argument contained in a familial analogy as a justification for obedience:

Since you were brought into the world and nurtured and educated by us, can you deny in the first place that you are our child and slave, as your fathers were before you? And if this is true, you are not on equal terms with us; nor can you think that you have a right to do to us what we are doing to you. Would you have any right to strike or revile or do any other evil to your father or your master, if you had one, because you have been struck or reviled by him, or received some other evil at his hands?[4]

The state has raised Socrates. It can make the same claims that a parent makes to a recalcitrant child. In fact, since in Plato's view the state has made it possible for parents to bring up children ("In the first place did we not bring you into existence? Your father married your mother by our aid and begat you"), it holds a claim to obedience prior to the family.[5]

If we now take this position of Plato's ("If he may do no violence to his father or mother much less may he do violence to his country"), we can see that the contract provides a very different function in his account of political obligation. The Athenian government does not "rudely impose" these benefits: "if [a citizen] does not like us when he has become of age . . . he may go where he pleases and take his goods with him."[6] Socrates clearly accepted these benefits by his residency, and the laws take Socrates' decision to raise his children in Athens as further "proof of his satisfaction." The contract, at least in this argument, is used to insure that the benefits offered by the state have been accepted. In Plato's previous argument it was the contract itself that constituted obligation. In fact, it is possible to state Plato's position in regard to Socrates' obligations without reference to a contract at all:

1. Benefits received create obligations to the giver.

2. Residence is equivalent to receipt of benefits.

3. Socrates is a resident.

4. Socrates is obliged to obey.

It is now easier to see why Plato is able to say with some plausibility that Socrates' disobedience would be such a serious affront to the state. Socrates would not have been a breaker of promises but an ingrate. He would have been a man who turned his back, not on the promises he had made, but on "a share in every good which [the state] had to give."[7] It is on these terms, and only these terms, that Plato is able to say that the state is "to be soothed, and gently and reverently entreated when angry, even more than a father, and either to be persuaded, or if not persuaded, to be obeyed."[8] No writer, not even one as audacious as Plato, could describe the state in this manner with a vocabulary of promising.

Thomas Hobbes, while no less an authoritarian than Plato, divests the state of all organic claims and for these reasons alone deserves his reputation as an incipient liberal. Yet because Hobbes advances a contract theory with terms so unbalanced, little attention has been paid to his argument for obedience from gratitude. The contract which creates the *Leviathan* is wellknown, and more than one has attempted to deny its tenability. Our concern, however, rests with Hobbes's distinction between a commonwealth by institution and commonwealth by acquisition. But before we can appreciate the significance of this distinction, we need to look at Hobbes's fourth law of nature.

The first and second laws of nature set the terms for civil peace. The third ("Men performe their Covenants made") provides the mechanism to insure a lasting order. Hobbes is understandably adamant about the importance of contracts. It is this law of nature which provides the "Fountain and Originall of Justice." More important for our purposes is Hobbes's contention that "where no Covenant hath preceded, there hath no Right been transferred, and every man has right to everything; and consequently, no action can be Unjust."[9] It would appear that the contract model exhausts the account of the political obligation in the *Leviathan*. But only a few lines later Hobbes outlines the fourth law of nature, "that a man which receiveth Benefit from another of meer grace, Endeavor that he that giveth it, have no reasonable cause to repent him of his good will."[10] The breach of this law is "called Ingratitude and hath the same relation to grace, that Injustice hath to Obligation by Covenant."[11]

Given Hobbes's clarity, the question arises why so few writers have spoken of obedience from gratitude in the *Leviathan*. One answer is that since Hobbes's justification of obedience from gratitude is virtually identical to his justification of obedience from contract, it is not easy to distinguish them. Both principles are derived from man's fear of death and his desire to secure peace. Without an obligation to keep promises, "convenants are in vain, and but empty words . . . and wee are still in the condition of Warre."[12] While gratitude depends upon "antecedent grace," "no man giveth, but with the intention of good to himselfe."[13] If men failed to express gratitude there would be "no beginning of benevolence, or trust nor consequently of mutuall help, nor reconciliation of one man to another and therefore they are to remain the condition of war."[14] Another answer is that after Hobbes makes the argument for an obligation to express gratitude he never attempts to use it in his account of political obligation (or so it would seem).

Political power occurs in two ways for Hobbes, commonwealth by institution and commonwealth by acquisition. The former case arises when "men agree to submit to some Man, or Assembly of Men," and it is upon this account that Hobbes's reputation as a political theorist rests. It is the latter that, while stated in the language of the contract model, is a surrogate for a theory of political obligation based upon gratitude. Hobbes contends that commonwealth by acquisition is not significantly different from that of institution. In both cases men act from fear; in the latter "for fear of one another," in the former "they subject themselves to him they are afraid of."[15] It is at this point that it appears that Hobbes meets the fate of all contract theorists by relying upon some notion of contract which affronts our common sense. In fact, Hobbes's solution looks even harsher than the one offered by Plato:

1. Contracts are obligatory.

2. Submission is equivalent to a contract.

3. One who submits is obliged.

If we examine Hobbes's two examples of commonwealth by institution, however, we can see that again there are dual theories of political obligation being presented to us. We are told that dominion is acquired in two ways, by generation and by conquest. By generation Hobbes is referring to the right of a parent over his child. His explanation of the child's duty is worth noting: "Seeing the Infant is first in the power of the Mother, so as she may either nourish, or expose it, if she nourish it, it oweth its life to the Mother . . . if she expose it, and another find, and nourish it, the Dominion is in him that nourish it."[16] Hobbes defends the inclusion of this sort of reasoning to the contract model by arguing that "every man is supposed to promise obedience, to him, in whose power it is to save, or destroy him."[17] Dominion by generation then is justified according to the third rather than the fourth law of nature. Yet since Hobbes defines gratitude in terms of antecedent grace, it would seem that parental authority could be at least as effectively justified by a benefits-received theory. Both the mother *and* the conqueror have no obligation to save their respective babies or prisoners. To the extent that they do so, the beneficiary could be considered obliged not to cause the former "to repent him of his good will." Moreover, Hobbes contends that in the case of dominion by conquest, the vanquished asks for quarter to "evade the present fury of the Victor" and that he does not give up his life as in the case of slavery, but has it "deffered till farther deliberation."[18] Yet if we compare Hobbes's treatment of grace in his discussion of the contract, one finds that on Hobbes's own terms the gratitude model is the appropriate application to commonwealth by acquisition:

When the transferring of Right, is not mutual; but one of the parties transferreth, in hope to gain thereby friendship or service from another, or from his friends; or in hope to gain the reputation of Charity, or Magnanimity; or to deliver his mind from the pain of compassion; or in hope of reward in heaven; this is not Contract, but *GIFT, FREE-GIFT, GRACE*: which words signifie one and the same thing.[19]

Commonwealth by acquisition fails to meet the requirements for inclusion into the contract model at both ends of the transaction: not only is the transfer of right not mutual, but no right (in terms of the vanquished) in Hobbes's terms exists in the first place. In fact, only after submission can it be said that the vanquished has a right and this only involves the *expectation* that the taking of his life has been deferred till further deliberation.

It is not terribly difficult to determine why Hobbes refused to consider a justification of commonwealth by acquisition which would both have been more consistent with the conception of contract he outlined earlier and have been more consistent with a reader's common sense. His problem involved providing a justification for obedience as strong as his justification offered in commonwealth by institution. Yet it was necessary that this other instance of political authority be strong in two senses. Hobbes seems to have felt that a theory of political obligation must not only weight the terms and interpretation of the terms in favor of the sovereign but that these terms and their interpretation must be authorized by the subject himself. By justifying dominion by conquest through a contract model, Hobbes is able to fulfill both his purposes:

The Master of the Servant, is Master also of all he hath; and may exact the use thereof; that is to say, of his goods, of his labour, of his servants, and of his children, as often as he shall think fit. For he holdeth his life of his Master, by the covenant of obedience; that is, of owning, and authorising whatsoever the Master shall do. *And in the case of the Master, if he refuse, kill him, or cast him into bonds, or otherwise punish him for his disobedience, he is himselfe the author of the same; and cannot accuse him of injury* [emphasis mine].[20]

We are informed that "it is not the Victory, that giveth the right of Dominion over the Vanquished, but his own Covenant."[21]

Had Hobbes viewed the position of the vanquished otherwise, he would on his own admission be forced to conclude that "such men . . . have no obligation at all; but may break their bonds, or the prison; and kill, or

carry away their Master, justly."[22] Had he seen the
vanquished as owing a debt of gratitude to the victor
for having spared his life, he would have been forced
to admonish the captive to give the victor "no reasonable
cause to repent him of his good will." An obligation of
this sort would seem to be a considerable one, but apparently it was not enough for Hobbes. This is not to
say that Hobbes did not pay a price for his selections.
The plausibility of his contract model is greatly enhanced
by the tendency of the reader to accept unconsciously
a parallel and supplementary theory based upon gratitude.
Hobbes encourages this acceptance when it suits his
purposes (as in the case of dominion by generation) and
discourages it when it does not (as in the instance of
dominion by conquest). But these tactics do not contribute
to "firme and lasting edifice" of reason which Hobbes
hoped would lead men to accept his political recommendations.

If one is about to conclude that the surrogate gratitude
model is only a device of authoritarian political thinkers,
let us examine the arguments of the classic natural rights
liberalism found in Locke's *Second Treatise*. Locke's
work is especially instructive in terms of the problem we
are discussing because fully two-thirds of the treatises are
a refutation of the paternal view of political authority
so congenial to the development of a gratitude theory
of political obligation. The *First Treatise* deals with the
more literal version of paternalism as developed in the
patriarchalism of Sir Robert Filmer. Locke challenges
this position by contending that if obedience to paternal
authority constitutes obedience to political authority, men
owe disobedience to only one authority, and since the
direct descendent of Adam is unknown, the doctrine of
patriarchalism "cuts up all government by the Roots."[23]

The *Second Treatise* begins with the announcement that the assorted relationships which exist in any society require identification separately. Different obligations may be appropriate to different social roles:

The first Society was between Man and Wife, which gave beginning to that between Parents and Children; to which, in time, that between Master and Servant came to be added: And through all these might, and commonly did meet together, and make up one Family, where in the Master or Mistress of it had some sort of Rule proper to a Family; each of these, or all together came short of Political Society, as we Shall see, if we consider the different Ends, Tyes and Bonds of each of these.[24]

Locke's method for considering the "Ends, Tyes and Bonds" of various sorts of human relationships is to construct the conditions under which they arise. In doing so, Locke frequently employs abstract structured environments in which other relations are, for the moment, deliberately left unconsidered. Such an approach, while it often leads to brilliant insights into the character of obligations, presents the reader with a confusing amalgam of genetic, teleological, and abstract ideal-type thinking. The state of nature, the device from which Locke works out most of the general moral obligations that men hold toward one another, becomes an historical construct, an explanatory abstraction, and a device heavy with teleological argumentation.

But Locke's basis of attack on paternalism is managed by examining "conjugal society" apart from political institutions. First he contends that it is God who is the author of the birth of children, and the child remains beholden to God through the laws of nature and not directly to his parents.[25] Fatherhood does involve duty but this is limited to the preservation of offspring, and Locke makes it clear that a child owes allegiance to whoever cares for him, regardless of parenthood.[26] The power of the parent is "temporary" and "reaches not to the Life and Property of the Child."[27] In fact, while Locke contends that a man owes duties to his parents after childhood, these are obligations of attitude not command: "Tis one thing to owe honour, respect, gratitude and assistance; another to require an absolute obedience and submission. The honour due to Parents, a Monarch in his Throne owes his Mother, and yet this lessens not his authority, nor subjects him to her government."[28]

Thus it is not so much fatherhood as such that demands the obedience of children and their honor in later years but performance of certain duties on the part of a parent. While Locke suggests that obligations may continue after childhood in hope of receiving the father's property, the basis of this action is hope of reward, not the virtue of fatherhood.[29] Even contracts (including the social contract) entered into by a parent are not binding upon the child. But we shall return to this important position shortly.

While Locke's target, the doctrine of patriarchalism by divine right, held that parenthood provided the character of a citizen's obligations to the state, it is entirely possible to contend separately that the state's relation to the citizenry is one of parent to child. Locke turned directly to this position and, even while conceding that the origins of the state lay in paternal power, attempted to refute the argument. His method of attack was similar to his positions on parental power. The whole purpose of fatherhood was to create the rational citizen: "To turn him loose to an unrestrain'd Liberty, before he has Reason to guide him, is not the allowing him the priviledge of his Nature, to be free; but to thrust him out amongst Brutes, and abandon him to a state as wretched, and as much beneath that of a Man, as theirs. This is that which puts the authority into the Parents' hands to govern the Minority of their Children."[30] Thus the parent plays a crucial role in educating men who will recognize their obligations. But familial and political authority are, by this very position, distinguished. For if the parent has done his job well, the state has no business to oversee the citizenry. A child come of age is a free man and by freedom Locke means "the liberty to dispose and order" his "Person, Actions, Possessions within the law" and "not to be subject to the arbitrary will of another."[31] Locke's insistence upon the capacity of man to recognize freely his obligations and act upon them makes the state as parent a logical impossibility.

The Filmerian argument for patriarchalism is a genetic one, and Locke, while he refuses to accept this method of justification in general, is willing to concede its anthropology. He accepts the contention that the beginning of political society was patriarchal but refuses to accept the corollary which says that allegiance is required because the head of state is a patriarch. The foundation of loyalty is consent. It may well be that in primitive societies paternal authority was commonly construed as political, yet "this was not by any Paternal Right, but only by the Consent of his Children."[32] Locke at this point concedes a good deal to the patriarchal system by admitting that such a form of government was well suited to the inexperienced and simple.[33] But from a strictly logical point of view Locke seems to be saying that the incidence of patriarchs in history gives no more weight to authority than had men originally chosen redheads to rule them. It is the process by which men create authority that *establishes* obligation not the characteristics of the men chosen. This is no mean point for a man to make in an age firmly riveted to a patriarchal explanation of duty.

With the current model of paternalism and the battery of images associated with it so firmly rejected, Locke faces the formidable task of constructing an alternate theory of political obligation. The doctrine of consent which emerges from subsequent chapters of the *Second Treatise* is Locke's now well-known alternative. We have examined the problems associated with this account in our last chapter. Yet what is so significant about the two versions of consent theory offered by Locke is that they allow for many of the same arguments of paternalism just disputed by the author. Express consent, the vehicle which creates "perfect" subjects to political authority, provides us with standards to judge the authority of government even if we ultimately reject the model as an inappropriate framework altogether. The action is voluntary, explicit and socially observable:

1. Contracts are obligatory.

2. Contracts are "actual agreements," "Express Declarations," "positive engagements."[34]

3. "A" has "declared."

4. "A" is obligated.

Tacit consent, however, introduces a phantom. If a contract can exist when there is an "Express Declaration" and when there is "no express declaration at all," the significance of the latter rests only with its limited claim. Locke tells us that *tacit* consent binds only with the enjoyment of the benefits of an *express* consent! For a writer who was so concerned to separate duties of men in society and carefully examine their origin, this fusion is especially puzzling. For Locke could have made the same argument that Plato and Hobbes refused to use as well:

1. Benefits create obligations on the part of the recipient.

2. Residence entails benefits given by the state.

3. "A" resides in a state.

4. "A" is obligated.

C. B. MacPherson has suggested that the tacit consent model was intended to assure the loyalty of a propertyless proletariat to a liberal political system. Yet a benefits theory would have attached the proletariat to the state as well as the consent theory. After all, the benefits required by Locke to produce obligations are slight enough. What the tacit consent theory does permit Locke to do that would not be available to him otherwise is to offer an account of political obligation which apparently refuses to borrow from the patriarchal model while at the same time employs patriarchal arguments for its plausibility. It is not the benefits then that the state bestows upon its subjects which create obligations, it is the tacit acceptance of the subject which characterizes one's duties to the state. Admittedly the distinction between the two theories at this point is very thin, but it was enough for Locke to avoid the presuppositions of patriarchalism. An openly stated benefits-received theory, with its congeniality to a gratitude relationship between subject and crown, leaves the subject very close to the position represented by Filmer. The selection of which benefits shall be bestowed upon the citizenry rests with the state, as it does with the parent, and the citizen is then called upon to express his gratitude through obedience to the gifts offered or to plead for greater generosity. Locke felt that consent theory altered the existing structure between citizen and state by placing the initial distribution of political goods with the citizen. When current practice did not reflect consent theory, as in the case of those who made "no expression at all" in modern polities and whole bodies primitive societies, Locke insisted upon submerging a possible gratitude relationship within the consent model. Locke, and perhaps the liberal tradition as well, did not really bury paternalism but disguised it with the mask of tacit consent.

The structure of gratitude

The fact that a theory of gratitude can be found in theorists as diverse as Plato, Hobbes, and Locke should not surprise the student of political obligation. The major difficulty in providing a justification of political authority rests upon the need to provide first a symmetry between moral and political action and then to present a plausible linkage between the two. One way this can be achieved is by defining morality in such a way as to make it comparable to currently accepted conceptions of politics. This appears to be the avenue taken by writers like Jean Jacques Rousseau and Friedrich Hegel. If one uses this approach the individual's relationship to his state can be determined by the telos already built into the author's model of ethics. Thus, Rousseau's account of the purpose of morality as the avoidance of *amour propre* through a head-first leap into community life actually requires the existence of political order. Hegel manages the same effect by viewing morality as an historical dialectic independent of the individual and conveniently reposed, if perhaps only for the moment, in the idea of the nation state.

Yet taking the concept of morality totally out of the arena of the individual moral judgment so affronts auxiliary concepts of ethics like responsibility and volition that few theorists wish to present a perfect symmetry. This may be why the contract/consent model has found such a universal appeal in recent history. By conceiving morality as a network of contracts, writers can treat the existence of political orders as volitional and intentional as well as independent of the continued evaluation of the duties one might owe to the state. Yet for all the advantages which the contract/consent model offers to the problem of political obligation, the theory nevertheless manages to achieve the consistency it enjoys in merging the requirements of moral and political action by raping the reality of political life. The problem becomes especially acute for liberal theorists since they are unwilling to posit any legitimate social order independent of consent. But the insistence of each theorist under discussion that residence is equivalent to the moral force of a promise is only made plausible by introducing non-contractarian criteria for recognizing moral duty and subsuming them under the contract model. What makes all these efforts more difficult to unravel is that the concept of gratitude is closely related to the concept of contract as a *via media* to an assumption of an obligation. Yet one of its most significant differences lies in the fact that the assumption of an obligation is out of the hands of the receiver of a benefit. One cannot refuse to pay a debt of gratitude because when drowning he did not contract with his rescuer to save him. Only by attempting to set out the structure of gratitude (when do we owe it, why do we owe it, and when is the debt paid?) can we be in a position to judge its utility for an account of political obligation.

In order to find out what gratitude involves, it is unfortunately necessary to present a sketch of prima facie rights and duties on the basis of how they are assumed. I move on here with considerable trepidation because I do not wish to suggest that I am offering any particular ethical theory. In fact, I hope the reader will accept the contention that the concepts discussed below are metaethical ones and not dependent upon any particular moral theory:

1. *Rights and duties arising from accepting the position of a moral actor.* Most moral philosophers seem to agree that the *homo ethicus* has (prima facie) duties of truth telling, promise keeping, beneficence, respect for others.

2. *Rights and duties arising from contracts and promises.* While the obligation to keep a promise is the result of 1, one who undertakes a promise assumes a special moral role since had he not promised, he presumably would be under no obligation to the party involved. While it is common to promise to do things which are part of the duties described in 1, this serves only to announce and/or emphasize that one occupies the general role of a moral actor.

3. *Rights and duties arising independently of contracts and the ordinary demands of accepting the position of a moral actor.* I have in mind here duties which result from "special bonds" among human beings. Different institutional arrangements in societies may lead different individuals or sets of individuals to share common situations. The relationship between parent and child, husband and wife (or

lovers in general), and friends is the result of a web of shared interests, experiences, past favors, and even mistakes.

While it is true that some of these relationships in 3 are treated by the law in contractual terms for the protection of both parties, a strong case can be made for an account of these allegiances in other than a contractual framework. In fact it is upon the reflection of these "special bonds" that often moves marriage partners to reconcile, parents to forgive errant children, and friends to help one another in distress. In most societies the best examples of these obligations are to be found in "blood relationships" because it is in the context of the family that joys and tragedies are shared. But "old army buddies" recognize the same sorts of obligations as well. The duties arising from "special bonds" are, of course, at the base of theories of patriotism. Admittedly more vague and consequently misunderstood, perceived duties to one's country often arise from an appreciation for one's friends and family. Yet the movement from a recognition of duty to the neighborhood doctor and proprietor of the corner grocery store to a recognition of duty to defend one's country is far from the logical transition that many would like to believe. In any case, it is those who are willing to forgive a brother-in-law's indiscretions who often use the same reasoning to overlook their country's errors as well. But, more important from our point of view, both decisions can be reached without recourse to promises or contracts.

Before we can begin an analysis of gratitude it is important that we do not forget an often neglected aspect of ethics. While each of the kinds of duties mentioned above are right to do and it is blameworthy to fail to them, there are a whole category of actions well in the arena of moral life which do not involve claims of duty or rights or blame at all. Called by modern moral philosophers supererogatory acts, these can be described as actions which are praiseworthy but not worthy of blame for those who fail to engage in them.[36] The layman would refer to people who perform such actions as saints or heroes. No one would blame as soldier who did not go behind enemy lines to destroy a closely guarded bridge without orders to do so but we do give honors to those who dare. Nor would we criticize a person who did not attempt to save a drowning man in hurricane waters but we would praise him if he chose to do so. Similarly, we would not chastize a doctor who chose not to spend a lifetime in a leper colony but we might cannonize the one who did after he were dead.

Yet despite these cases of sainthood and heroism, the concept of supererogatory moral acts, especially in terms of their relationship to acts of moral duty, is not always capable of clear definition. Are acts of beneficence supererogatory acts? Many moral philosophers have suggested that they are. Is beneficence to be expected by another moral agent and is blame to be parceled out when it is not forthcoming? Or is helping others a supererogatory act which should be praised but not a part of one's moral duty. Kant claimed that if we were to accept the right to beneficence then the concept of gratitude would have no place in ethics since a person need not thank another for respecting his rights. And who would not think at least a word of thanks is owed from a rescued swimmer? Rousseau felt that the concept of gratitude was so puzzling on this point that he claimed it involved a paradox: "What kind of debt can the debtor owe and yet the creditor be expected to disclaim? The debt of gratitude."

But a good deal of the confusion about moral duty and beneficence and gratitude can be eliminated if we sort out its causes. Part of the problem results from the fact that moral courses of action do not exhaust the range of human alternatives and that in fact the moral life involves an extremely fragile set of experiences. Thus when we thank profusely someone who has returned our wallet, this need not mean that the finder did not have an obligation to return something which was not his but that we are overwhelmed by the fact that someone has chosen to act according to moral precepts. There are, of course, some very difficult cases in which the distinction between acts of duty and supererogatory acts are difficult to discern.[37] These instances are not unimportant and it is worthwhile to consider the lines between cowardice and caution or heroism and recklessness. But the essence of moral life is not nearly so complicated. Just as it is unthinkable that an apartment dweller not telephone the police when he sees a mugging outside his window, in so far as we are willing to speak in moral terms, we are unavoidably let to presume a prima facie duty to help others. Whether the apartment dweller should have shouted out the window or run to the street in aid we can leave to dramatists.

But if beneficence is a moral duty how can we tell when gratitude is owed? That is, how do we know when to thank someone when he has acted beyond the requirements of duty? Some help in this matter can be found by examining the argument of a recent paper on gratitude. In his "Odd Debt of Gratitude," Daniel Lyons incorporates the concept of gratitude into what we have referred to as supererogatory acts: "Real thanks are due to A for helping B insofar as this help is 'really' praiseworthy, and insofar as blaming A would be inappropriate for failing to help B."[38] Lyons distinguishes "real" thanks from "perfunctory" thanks. The latter occurs when the man to be thanked is expected to wave away the thanks or is out of order in insisting upon real thanks. Lyons employs a cost-benefit, analysis to determine if gratitude is actually owed. For example, if A saw B drowning and was able to save him by casting a rope into the water, we could say that the cost to A in time and energy was far less than the benefit to B and therefore A performed a fairly uniform discharge of his duty of beneficence. But if A risked his own life by jumping into turbulent water to save B, it would seem that B did indeed owe A a debt of gratitude. Lyons's calculus even allows us to account for differences in individual ability in determining duties of beneficence. If A were an Olympic gold medal winner the cost to him would be less than if he were an average swimmer or if he could not swim at all.

In sum, Lyons suggests that gratitude is due when the cost to the agent is less than the benefit to the recipient.[39] We will not accept this calculus as a basis for a theory of gratitude since its utilitarian framework does create some objectionable and unnecessary problems. But Lyons's analysis does establish a place for gratitude in moral relationships within a framework which recognizes a duty of beneficence.

If gratitude applies to only certain kinds of beneficent acts, supererogatory ones, we still must ask ourselves if it applies to acts arising from "contracts" or "special bonds." At first glance, the concept of gratitude appears unrelated to the performance of contracts or promises. One is not expected to be grateful to one who keeps his promise; he is merely doing his duty. If the action the promiser undertakes was especially dangerous (bringing the murderer of a friend to justice) , we might certainly owe thanks but not for the promise kept but for the decision to help which led to a promise. The reciprocal nature of contracts and the voluntary assumption of duties in promising does seem to make thanks appropriate. The problem does occur, however, in a set of important borderline cases. Do we owe gratitude to a fireman who saves our life? Are we justified in blaming a death on a fireman who refuses to enter the second floor of a building on fire? Do we blame a policeman for shooting at a threatening crowd? Do we thank him for overtaking an armed thief and recovering our life savings? In each of these cases we are speaking of persons occupying social roles more or less voluntarily undertaken in a contractual framework. Moreover, we are assuming a degree of professionalism which does not characterize the rest of the population. Therefore, it is not unreasonable to expect special skills in dangerous situations (such as the ability to avoid weak beams in a burning house, or to practice karate) as well as a lower panic point in extreme circumstances. Therefore we might be less willing to excuse cowardice and more willing to expect risk taking on the part of a fireman or a policeman both because bravery is part of the normal expectations of the role and the contract which formalizes it and because the possession of certain skills raises the number and kind of acts which we have come to regard as routine. But it does not follow that it is impossible to conceive of supererogatory acts for persons in these positions. Fire and police departments honor members for heroism and have standards designed to distinguish routine from extraordinary performance. In short certain contracted relationships do alter the line between acts of duty and spererogation but they do not eliminate the distinction altogether.

Our third class of moral duties, those arising from "special relationships," create duties which resemble debts of gratitude and in fact are very often confused with them. We indicated above that the most common example of special relationships is in the family. It is quite common for a parent to expect gratitude from a son and for a son to perceive a debt of gratitude to the parent. We have seen that Plato used these relationships in his theory of political obligation to suggest that familial gratitude ought to be displaced in favor of gratitude toward the state. Hobbes insisted that such gratitude arose from contract in spite of his earlier definitions. And Locke, while he makes an effort to minimize the political import of familial relationships, nevertheless recognizes gratitude as a duty owed to parents. If we assume that family members have duties toward one another more demanding than we might expect them to have toward strangers, can these plausibily be expressed as duties of gratitude? This is a question of some considerable importance since many regard themselves as standing in a special relationship to the state and perceive a debt of gratitude rising from that relationship. A whole network of duties commonly associated with parenthood are usually subsumed under the precept of providing for them material comfort, spiritual and intellectual development of the child. In fact the American middle-class parent has added an additional duty to his role — that of assuring that his offspring has a better life than himself. Why these duties are owed is of course a difficult question. But let us suggest this answer: We have contended that any person has a prima facie duty to help others. Since human offspring are the most helpless creatures, our obligations to them are clear and continuing. But if we have our duty to shelter a lost child or feed an infant as only a special case of our duty to help anyone, how can we account for more strongly felt duties to our children by birth? Let me suggest two replies, one very conventional and one tentative and naturalistic: (1) our own children are our special responsibility since we are originally responsible for their existence, (2) as societies are presently ogranized, the family provides an existing framework for the development of special relationships between persons, and practices which foster such are desirable.[40]

The duty of a son or daughter to his parents can be conceived then as duty not arising from gratitude but from the special relationship of which they are a part. If the sacrifice of a parent is part of the discharge of his duty, then the recipient of that sacrifice need not frame his duties in terms of gratitude. Similarly the duties of a son to his parents when the latter need help in their old age are the result of a special relationship they have enjoyed. They need not be judged as acts of supererogation requiring a debt of gratitude on the part of the elderly either, just as our moral duty to help all the aged arises from the principle of beneficence. All of this is not to suggest that acts of supererogation are not inconceivable in the parent/child relationship (just as they were not judged inappropriate in our discussion of contracts). Likewise, our duties are not totally open-ended, and there comes a time when we feel we can no longer indulge a friend or protect a son.

We have suggested that gratitude is owed only as a response to supererogatory acts and that the determination of a supererogatory act may vary according to the moral framework shared by the agents in question. But what exactly does the recipient of a supererogatory act owe? Suppose Baker saves Cane's life in combat

at great risk to his own life. We would certainly think
that Cane owes a debt of gratitude to Baker. But what
precisely deos he owe? Does he now have a duty:

1. to risk his life if appropriate circumstances arose?

2. to care for Baker if he should become disabled
or care for his children upon his death?

3. to respond to a petty request such as a five-dollar
loan?

4. to help Baker find a job after the war is over?

5. To perjure himself in court if he subsequently sees
Baker steal supplies from the PX?

6. participate in a robbery planned by Baker?

7. show his gratitude by a sincere word of thanks?

Under which circumstances would Cane's refusal force
us to judge him as an ingrate? Certainly a refusal to
respond in situations 3 and 7 would permit moral condemnation. Requests 2 and 4 are more demanding but
they would probably also fall under the debt of gratitude.
Options 1 and 5 are more difficult cases and may be impossible to decide without more detail and a long casuistic
analysis. In 5 Cane might feel an obligation to overlook
a petty theft if he felt it was not a part of a pattern (a
decision he would not be in a position to make had he
not been a partner in a special relationship with Baker).
One is a very troublesome request since it asks if receipt
of a supererogatory act makes supererogatory acts
obligatory on the part of the recipient. Perhaps we might
say that the failure to risk one's life for a man who has
risked his own for you would not involve blame on the
part of the moral community but could well involve guilt
on the part of the actor himself. Often the conscientious

moral actor is more harsh in parceling out blame to himself than he is to others. There may be good reasons for this sentiment. In the most trying moral situations only the participant himself possesses the combination of individual responsibility and self-examination necessary for honest evaluation. But in 6 we would be hard pressed to contend that Cane has an obligation to commit robbery out of gratitude to his benefactor. Supererogatory acts create duties of gratitude for their recipients but they do not alter completely the bounds of moral rightness.

Gratitude and political obligation

We are now in a position to assess the role that gratitude can play in contributing to an account of political obligation. Rather than restricting ourselves to the traditional preoccupation with the duties a citizen owes to his state, let us approach the problem in this framework: (1) gratitude the citizen owes the state; (2) gratitude the state owes the citizen; (3) gratitude the citizen owes other citizens.

If we consider the ordinary benefits a citizen receives in a relatively well ordered liberal democratic state in the twentieth century we might list the following: protection against aggression, schooling, highways, economic security, freedom to travel, speak, etc. A very common response to a questioning of one's duties to the state often proceeds along these lines: "Look at the freedom you have in this country, look at the educational system available to everyone, look at the standard of living you enjoy, don't you think you owe the state something?" Now there are, of course, a number of responses available to this question other than unequivocal agreement. One might challenge the existence, quality, and distribution of the benefits allegedly received. In fact, on these terms, particularly in regard to distributive justice in the industrial democracies, a benefits-received theory may be the least plausible justification for obedience. One may also challenge the source of the benefits themselves. Thoreau replies to an anticipated benefits-received theory in this fashion: "Yet this government never of itself furthered any enterprise, but by the alacrity with which it got out of its way. *It* does not keep the country free. *It* does not settle the West. *It* does not educate. The character inherent in the American people has done all that has been accomplished; and it would have done somewhat more if the government had not sometimes got in its way."[41] One need not go to this length, however, to assert that at least part of the benefits under discussion were indeed provided by the citizen himself. He in fact has paid the taxes that financed highway construction. He is a member of the PTA or a teacher himself. In short, he is being called upon to pay a debt of gratitude for a benefit that he has given to himself.

But if we approach the gratitude agreement head on, conceding that benefits have indeed been received, we will probably find that gratitude is still not a justifiable reason for obedience. For what the above piece of conventional wisdom asks us to say is this: I owe you a debt of gratitude for protecting my rights, for not stealing my money, and for generally acting justly. That is, the citizen is asked to be grateful when the state is doing its duty. It is equivalent to asking a person to be grateful to someone for not murdering him or stealing his wallet or libeling him. This is not to say that it is impossible for the state to perform supererogatory acts, acts worthy of such praise that they deserve a debt of gratitude. But it is terribly difficult to find an example of one in the real world. Ironically, however, a contract theory reduces the scope of acts which might be deserved to be called supererogatory. If the state is party to a contract which transforms it to a "watchman" or "umpire," then it must take the risks and abuse which are associated with these roles as a matter of course. Moreover, even if we could establish one, it does not follow if the reader accepts our discussion on the structure of gratitude that a debt of gratitude on the part of the citizen obliges him to do something for his benefactor which he thinks is morally wrong.

But can the state owe its citizenry a debt of gratitude? Can some of the things which the average citizen does like paying taxes, voting, participating in policy decisions be related to gratitude? Again there is a common line of reasoning which corresponds to this relationship: "I pay my taxes, stop at traffic lights, work hard for a living (and others do none of these things). The government owes a debt of gratitude to me and others like me." If indeed these are a partial listing of the duties of a citizen, then those who do not perform them deserve the condemnation of the citizen and perhaps the state. But if our preceding analysis was correct, the state is not obliged to respond out of gratitude toward those citizens who in Locke's words "do not quit their station willfully." When the citizen does perform supererogatory acts, a response on the part of the state should be forthcoming. There are two relatively common examples of such acts which might clarify our point. A citizen who shows valor on the battlefield or one who dedicates his whole life to public service deserves some special recognition by the state.[42] Committees organized after World War I claimed that a disabled soldier deserved the help of the state not out of a general duty of beneficence but from gratitude. Citizens who have made extraordinary contributions to public service are similarly recognized.[43]

A much more troublesome gratitude relationship exists between citizen and citizen. It is troublesome because it is often difficult in theory as well as practice to delineate clearly the duties one citizen owes to another from the duties being requested from him by the state which are justified in the name of the citizenry. Liberal political theorists have felt that maintenance of the distinction is crucial and have offered a conceptualization which divides the society from the state. In this tradition many of the duties one owes to another are either regarded as social or completely privatized. In the liberal society the duty of beneficence is recognized but rarely performed by men in their capacity as citizens nor is it discharged through the state. But even if we allow such a distinction, there are some requests in which the source of obligation is difficult to locate. Take the following argument which every male under thirty has heard: "I fought in World War II. I sacrificed four years of my life for my fellow citizens. Now I am too old to fight. I have discharged my obligations to the citizens of my generation and yours — now it is time for you to discharge your duty to me and your forebears."[44] Note that the argument is not directed at the citizen's duties to the homeland or to his obligation to obey the law but at one citizen's obligations to another. The structure of the argument is very much like one which a drowning man might make to a person he had once saved from death. We have indicated above the moral agony involved in such a request. Yet certainly the argument loses its force if the debtor denies the emergency or if he regards the request in this instance as immoral. But the most troublesome aspect of the situation is that a third party, the state, has created the obligation claim structure in the first place. Until the state is trusted, the gratitude claim on the part of fellow citizens remains clouded and dissolves into a claim between citizen and state.

Liberalism and gratitude

John C. Livingston and Robert G. Thompson have contended that despite the widely held acceptance of a pluralist theory of politics, pleas for restraint and order in a liberal society are couched in a Jeffersonian majority rule format.[45] Since pluralist theory places a premium on bargaining and contends that an automatic stabilization of interests is the result, it is unable to justify restraints when the bargaining tactic employed involves threats and coercion. Something of the same argument can be made in regard to the liberal state in general. Liberalism really offers only two accounts of political obligation, both broadly untilitarian. Obedience to the state is either justified on the basis of the contention that it is instrumental to the satisfaction of our needs or on the basis of a contract among citizens. It has always been one of the virtues of liberal thought to view politics in a tough no-nonsense fashion. From Hobbes through the pluralists, politics is regarded as a bitter, dangerous struggle over conflicting interests leading liberals to treat the state as a potential oppressor. And while it is not necessary here to discuss the numerous devices which have been employed to avoid that end, it is safe to say that the recourse in justifying political action has nearly always been to submit policies to the cold calculations of the utility principle. But since the state is not to be regarded as a friend much less a father, it is difficult to request extreme sacrifice from a liberal citizenry. Edmund Burke challenged the liberal mind on this point when he said this to the House of Commons:

Do you imagine, then, that it is the Land Tax Act which raises your revenue? That it is the annual vote in the Committe of supply, which gives you your army? Or that it is the mutiny bill which inspired it with bravery and discipline? No! Surely no. It is the love of the people; it is their attachment to their government, from the sense of the deep stake that they have in such a glorius institution, which gives you your army and your navy and infuses into both that liberal obedience without which your army would be a base rabble and your navy nothing but rotten timber.46

This is not to say that liberal governments have not employed nonliberal motivations for obedience. They have and they have done so with some success. But they have done so by bringing them in through the back door. Abraham Lincoln's admonition to obedience before the Civil War infuses the contract model with a civil religion:

Let every American, every lover of liberty, every well wisher to his posterity, swear by the blood of the Revolution, never to viotate in the least particular, the laws of the country; and never to tolerate their violation by others. As the patriots of seventy-six did to the support of the Constitution and Laws, let every American pledge his life, property, and his sacred honor; let every man remember that to violate the law, is to trample on the blood of his father, and to tear the charter of his own and his children's liberty. Let reverence for the laws, be breathed by every American mother, to the lisping babe, that prattles on her lap — let it be taught in schools, in seminaries and in colleges; let it be written in Primers, spelling books, and in Almanacs; — let it be preached from the pulpit, proclaimed in legislative halls, and enforced in courts of justice. And, in short, let it become the political religion of the nation; and let the old and the young, the rich and the poor, the grave and the gay, of all sexes and tongues, and colors and conditions, sacrifice unceasingly upon its altars.47

President Lyndon B. Johnson tried frantically to unite

the special relationship ground for obedience of which we spoke with liberal theory:

> I know that in some quarters today patriotism is regarded with puzzlement or disdain.
> There are plentiful reasons for this. Many people feel a deep sense of rootlessness in the swirling currents of modern life. They are strangers to their neighbors and their community, and so they feel estranged from their country.
> To others, patriotism too often means patrioteering. It means concealing a world of error and wrong judgment beneath the flag. . . .
> Now let us say what we mean by the word — as simply as we know how. . . .
> We mean that love of peace, of comradeship and shared experience, of all the suffering and joy that really go to make up a people's history. . . . We mean that courageous love that sees in the oppression of other peoples a challenge to itself — and that reaches out to meet that challenge.[48]

The gratitude model has been a convenient vehicle for expressing the need for obedience rising out of a sense of community in a society which forbids its inclusion in a theory of political obligation. It formed the underlying structure of John Cotton's attack on Roger Williams and it remains as the basis for attacks on dissent today. Louis Hartz noted with alarm a comment by Sen. McCumber that Bolsheviks were "beasts."[49] Hartz attributes the remark to the cocoon-like ignorance of a liberal soiety to other modes of political organization and its often brutal responses when their existence is recognized. But what is so distressing about the remark is that there are not supposed to be any beasts at all, at least in an Aristotlean view, in a liberal society because there is no community in a political sense.[50]

Doubtless the concept of patriotism is difficult to express in liberal theory since it requires an emotional response to an organization that should ideally resemble a supermarket, dispensing political goods to the buyer routinely and fairly but without fanfare. In fact it has been the genius of liberalism to regard departures from sobriety in politics with suspicion. When patriotism rears its head in the liberal society it often takes the form of gratitude. We have suggested that when properly examined and separated from contractarian thought, gratitude fails as a general ground for obedience. But more important, it is a concept tacked onto liberal values. Not only does this process distort the values of liberalism but the patriotism which it involves is skewed and not fully understood even by its adherents.

None of these comments are meant to include this discusssion with the general onslaught against liberalism that is now in process in America. Perhaps liberal governments would do well to simply stop demanding the sort of sacrifices on the part of their citizenry which make the appeal to gratitude so tempting. In any case, the liberal has always insisted upon viewing politics under harsh analysis. In that spirit we are justified in saying that all concepts which are used to provide a link between moral duty and political obligation meet with only limited success, and perhaps the notion of gratitude fares no worse than any others. But because it is so easily hidden and confused with other moral duties and because it demands so much more in its performance, the concept of gratitude may do more harm than others in leading men to misplace their duties and to misjudge those who are so fortunate to find them.

5

Liberalism, Trust, and the Judicious Citizen

But if all the World shall observe Pretences of one kind, and Actions of another; Arts used to elude the Law, and the Trust of Prerogative . . . employed contrary to the end for which it is given . . . if a long Train of Actings shew the Councils all tending that way, how can a Man any more hinder himself from being persuaded in his own Mind. which way things are going?

—*John Locke*

OUR WRECKING OPERATION now appears to be complete. A serious attention to moral judgment forbids a moral theory of political obligation. Nor can the concepts of consent and gratitude hand up the moral autonomy of the citizenry to the state. But before we attempt to deal with the apparent irreconcilability between the notions of morality and political authority, it may be helpful to mention some of those who have come to the same conclusions as those reached in this essay. A wide variety of theorists have recognized at least in part that a theory of ethics which takes proper consideration of the role of moral judgment seriously damages the prospects for a model of moral duty providing for a theory of political obligation. They differ considerably, however, both in their reasons for this assessment and in the consequences their theories suggest might follow from it. And while no attempt is being made to suggest that the positions discussed below exhaust the current discussion of the subject, they do represent a major section of opinion on the subject and they may well be the legacy that twentieth-century political thought leaves to the problem of political obligation. More importantly, however, we shall see that since there are very serious problems in each of these positions, there is a need to offer a different approach.

One set of ethical theorists who have appreciated, although frequently in an oblique fashion, the position outlined in this essay have been the intuitionists. Always suspicious of moral theorizing, intuitionists have been at their best when criticizing competing moral and political philosophies. The contemporary intuitionist contribution to an account of political obligation is one result of its dogged pursuit of logical inconsistencies in utilitarian theory. In 1935 H. A. Prichard, one of the most brilliant of modern intuitionists, attacked T. H. Green's *Principles of Political Obligation*. It has been this critique which has had an enormous influence upon treatment of the concept of political obligation even though few writers have accepted the moral theory which supported his analysis. Prichard begins like most theorists in seeing political obligation as a part of a general theory of moral obligation:

The question [Why is it the duty of a subject to obey his ruler?], it should be noted, is similar to questions about acts of other kinds which we ordinarily think of as duties, such as, why ought we to speak truthfully or to consider the feelings of others? Hence an answer is really only part of a theory of Moral Obligation in general (viz., that part which concerns one special obligation) and unless we recognize this, we are apt to go astray in looking for the answer.[1]

He was objecting only to the model of moral obligation which Green had used: "Underlying the lectures is a peculiar theory of Moral Obligation which is totally inconsistent with our ordinary moral ideas."[2] Prichard's theory of morals contended that there are no principles or rules which can be applied to moral decision making. A man may know what is morally required of him but any attempts at justifying this decision by moral or nonmoral rules are bound to lead him not only to confusion, but to immoral conduct in the future. Prichard's justification for this position is the time-honored paradox of moral rules: "Now consideration of instances of what seem conflicting duties is enough to show that no kind of action whatever can, strictly speaking, be a duty, if only for the reason that if it were, there might be occasions on which we are bound to do two actions, although we could only do one or the other of them."[3] We will not now bother to refute this argument, although it seems clear on reflection that duties need not be left in an unconnected heap in order to still be called duties. The point, however, is that Green's error on Prichard's terms lay in "making the mistake of putting forward as *the* ground what is a ground of political obligation."[4] Prichard contended that "because the thing called a state may in each case be different, and if there are kinds of states, the ground of duty to obey may depend on the kind."[5] We are told that the question as to political obligation as it had been formulated is the same as the question "Why ought we to read books?" the question about reading books is not a "proper question, so long as we are considering books generally, as distinct from books of a particular sort."[6] Prichard concludes by offering two substitute questions for the original one: Why ought subjects of certain specified sorts of governments to obey them? And does this claim to obey outweigh other possible claims?

Prichard had denied the validity of Green's argument because one standard of moral conduct (utilitarianism) had been used to evaluate a variety of political systems. The use of sets of rules to evaluate either personal conduct or political institutions violated the intuitionists' belief that all human situations can only be understood in concrete and unique terms. As such, a question as general as "Why ought I obey the state?" had to be considered inappropriate. Just as important for our purposes, however, is Prichard's acceptance of political obligation as an aspect of moral duty.[7]

While the intuitionists have been persistent and often effective critics of the numerous moral theories of political obligation, their influence upon political theory has been restricted precisely because of their own analysis. That is, the intuitionist critique remains plausible only in the context of their own theory of ethics. And in a secular age in which political as well as moral justification is almost invariably functional or teleological, the intuitionist has had the unhappy task of offering a view of moral judgments which by his own definition is not subject to anything but a reductio ad adsurdum proof.

But what is so intriguing about the history of contemporary ideas of political obligation is that the successors to the intuitionists as the dominant school of ethical theory, the noncognitivists, have made use of the critique of political obligation discussed above without feeling the necessity of bother with a defense of their own theory of ethics. The noncognitivists theory of ethics, which every political scientist knows by heart if not by name, contends that since moral judgments are expressions of the sentiments or beliefs of the holder, they are neither true nor false. What many political scientists do not know, however, is that ethical noncognitivism is a broad position which includes numerous and complex variations congenial to various political recommendations.[8] Many noncognitivists, however, are agreed that there is little utility in the concept of political obligation as traditionally formulated.[9]

One of the earliest attempts to apply this position to the concept of political obligation can be found in an analysis by Margaret MacDonald. In a paper delivered to the Aristotelian Society in 1940, MacDonald argued that upon careful examination the question "Why ought I obey the state?"[10] dissolved into a philosophical error. Noting that so "many important words used in political discussion have a degree of vagueness which make it even easier in political than in other branches of philosophy to disguise a linguistic elucidation or recommendation as an important factual discovery," she claimed that the task of a political philosopher was to determine how far questions are empirical and to what extent they are linguistic.

MacDonald used a decidedly noncognitivist position, albeit a remarkably moderate one, to arrive at her judgment about the concept of political obligation. She contended that although philosophical questions about politics "predict nothing about behavior" and are "empty of factual content," there is a "point" to these remarks. The theories of political obligation offered by traditional political philosophers, consent, tradition, objects promoted, are important standards to apply in determining why one ought to obey the state, but each is not important on every occasion. Adherence to the performance of one standard would lead to a decision about one's obligations which challenge our intuitive standards of what we think we ought to do. Governments may promote certain social goods and still be autocratic. While MacDonald momentarily flirted with duration of absence as a justification of resistance to political authority, she quickly reasserted her position that "the manner in which they (and probably others) are blended is infinitely various and no precise definition could describe one usage." She concludes that it should not be surprising that a general answer to the question which political obligation raises is neither possible nor necessary: "A general proof of the existence of material objects seems impossible, and to ask for it, absurd. No general criterion of all right actions can be supplied. Similarly, the answer to "Why should I obey *any* law, acknowledge the authority of *any* state or support *any* government?" is that this is a senseless question.'[11]' The essay concludes by saying that the value of traditional political theories lies not in the general information they give about the basis of political obligation but in their skill in emphasizing at a critical moment a criterion which is tending to be overlooked or denied. No necessary and sufficient ground of political obligation is to be formed; the only answerable question which the issue of political obligation raises is "Why should I obey this government under these circumstances?"

MacDonald left a small but, to her mind, important place for the consideration of political obligation as traditionally formulated. Other writers in the same tradition have been more adamant. In a recent book, Thomas McPherson has suggested an even more drastic revision.[12] McPherson's argument for a moratorium on discussion of political obligation as he understands it is a complicated one. However, the core of his argument is very similar to MacDonald's and can be stated simply. What McPherson objects to is the "moralizing" about politics that has been the preoccupation of traditional political philosophies: "The very use of the term 'obligation' . . . suggests that moral matters may be involved. Clearly, there are moral questions about politics, but I believe philosophers have been altogether too ready to look at political obligation from a narrowly moral point of view."[13] For McPherson moral obligation is understood in noncognitivist terms; we are obliged when we "feel moral approval." For some citizens paying taxes involves fulfillment of moral obligations; for others it does not. Given both the individuality and internality of morality, no general theory of political obligation can be provided:

A political philosophy can be contracted that neither makes explicit use of this concept nor requires it. Such have been contracted. Certain writers have, it is true, felt bound to use the notion of political obligation, but it is so general a notion as to do little or no useful work, and if interpreted in terms specific enough to be useful it is . . . no longer the satisfyingly general thing that those writers wanted in the first place.[14]

In addition McPherson offers an observation noted earlier in this paper as well. He contends that the "moralizing of politics is not on the whole true to the practice of governments themselves": "'Do this' or 'this is expedient' is the sense of government commands or pronouncements, rather than 'you ought to do this.'"[15] While this discrepancy leads McPherson to question the utility of the concept of political obligation, it has led others to question the utility of government itself.

Anarchists, for instance, can claim a long tradition

for advancing the most exacting relationship between ethics and politics. While some anarchists have not been careful to observe that relationship when promoting their ideal, they steadfastly deny that the state possesses any any moral status whatsoever. This position has been most recently advanced by Robert Paul Wolff in his *In Defense of Anarchism*. The appeal of Wolff's book often lies more in his overall honesty and poignancy than in the plausibility of its arguments. Yet part of Wolff's argument is very similar to the conclusion reached about conscience earlier in this essay:

> The responsible man is not capricious or anarchic, for he does acknowledge himself bound by moral constraints. But he insists that he alone is the judge of those constraints. He may listen to the advice of others, but he makes it his own by determining for himself whether it is good advice. He may learn from others about his moral obligations, but only in the sense that a mathematician learns from other mathematicians — namely by hearing from them arguments whose validity he recognizes even though he did not think of them himself. He does not learn in the sense that one learns from an explorer, by accepting as true his accounts of things one cannot see for oneself . . . . The autonomous man, insofar as he is autonomous, is not subject to the will of another. He may do what another tells him, but not because he has been told to do it.[16]

On these terms, the concept of command is inconsistent with the concept of morality (or in Wolff's usage, moral autonomy) . For Wolff consequences of this position are clear: all political authority is morally unjustifiable *and* "philosophical anarchism would seem to be the only reasonable political belief for an enlightened man."[17] The latter conclusion, however, is justified only by Wolff's conception of political philosophy as a "dependent or derivative discipline (of ethics) : "The normative concept of the state as the human community which possesses rightful authority within a territory . . . defines the subject matter of political philosophy proper."[18] And while Wolff recognizes that is is possible to raise moral questions about de facto states, he relegates this to the study of "casuistical politics." The "fundamental task" is to provide a deduction of the concept of the state.

A fourth position concerned with the question of political obligation is one most familiar to all of us, discussed at length in chapter 3. Consent theory regards the existence of states as compatible with the exercise of moral duty and yet insists that the traditional formulation of the question of political obligation is answerable. It attempts to formulate an answer within this framework both by insisting that the question of political obligation can only be answered in moral terms and by reducing moral duty to an account of the performance of a single act or to a single class of acts. Moral judgments are removed from the considerations of "What ought I do?" to the considerations "What did I promise, contract, or consent to do?"[19] Somehow individuals relinguish their states as moral agents, as men who perform obligations on the basis of whether it is right or wrong to do certain things. This new status is nevertheless consistent with morality because the decision to relinquish one's right to moral judgment is voluntary, done with full awareness of the consequences. Consent theorists have, however, been confronted with two related problems in justifying their position. They must necessarily regard moral obligations as arising solely from voluntary acts on the part of the agent. This led Hobbes to insist that the obligations of a child to a parent were contractual, led Locke to insist that the existence of coin exchange was based upon the consent of men, and led Tussman to insist that a sign, "No Smoking," be read as "We have agreed not to smoke here." And consent theorists must establish that consent has virtually been given.[20]

What all of these accounts have in common, of course, is the presupposition that political obligation is to be conceived in terms of some sort of moral reduction. That is, political obligation concerns the attempt to answer the question, "Why ought I *morally* to obey the state?" The intuitionist's conception of morality forbids a question of such generality and he therefore refuses to accept the concept itself. Similarly, the noncognitivist, by denying any cognitive status to moral statements, assumes that the subject of political obligation is "senseless" or unanswerable. The anarchist (or at least the variety of anarchism we have sampled) likewise accepts the premise that an answer to the problem of political obligation must be a moral one and concludes that no man owes obedience to political authority. And finally, the consent theorist is forced to construct a very restricted model of morality so that it can be made compatible with the requisites of political order.

We have argued in chapter 2 that moral judgment and political authority are incompatible categories of action, yet it need not follow that one accept the conclusions of the above positions. Although for probably very different reasons, none of the writers we have discussed have considered the possibility that the question "Why ought I obey the state?" can be given at least a partial answer without an assumption of an "ought" derived from a concept of moral duty.[21] None of what follows is meant to overcome the fatalism expressed by Locke in his recourse to the "Appeal to Heaven." It is meant, however, to offer an account of political obligation which both recognizes the realities of political power and at the same time insists upon the need for its moral evaluation.

We could, of course, like the anarchists, contend that men should obey the state only to the extent that they must. There is indeed a sense in which we say one "ought" and indeed is "obliged" to obey someone who orders us at gunpoint. If we accept this position, however, we are left to conclude that those states which have the most guns and use them most effectively are most deserving of our obligations. But there is an inescapable difference between a state with a secret police and forced labor camps and a state with a constitution and elections. The insight of the anarchist lies in showing us that the state is a shotgun behind the door. Yet the anarchist obscures the real task of political philosophy, and one that many liberals have perceived, which is to show how we can, as much as possible, keep that door shut. We must ask "Why obey the state?" while we recognize only too well that our answer will fall short of a theory of moral duty and yet rise above prudence.

This is a task not too unlike the one John Locke saw before him. Political authority was limited to an "express or tacit trust" that it be used for the "good [of the people] and the preservation of their Property."22 When it was "applied to other ends, and made use of to impoverish, harass, or subdue," it was tyranny "whether those that thus use it are the one or many."23 But while the people were the judge whether the prince or legislature acted contrary to their trust, if the state chose to ignore "that way of determination," the appeal lies nowhere but to heaven. Force between persons permitted "no Appeal to a Judge on Earth."24

Yet on Locke's terms, it was certainly possible to

evaluate the state morally. One was clearly obliged to the extent that he felt the governor's policies conformed to the law and could reasonably be expected to continue to do so, to the extent that government was legitimate. Both this assessment on the part of the citizen and the position of the state in society were characterized by Locke as an "express or tacit trust." The conclusion that one was obliged to obey the state to the extent that it could be trusted involved two basic restrictions on the governors according to Locke. The state must provide "promulgated standing Laws" so that "both the people may know their Duty . . . and the Rulers too kept within their due bounds."[25] When it became necessary to act in the absence of rules, or even contrary to them, the governors were to use their own discretion. Yet this prerogative existed at the pleasure of the citizenry who could eliminate or narrow it when it was exercised contrary to the public good. Locke was convinced that the people never challenged state discretion while it was "in any tolerable degree employed for the use it was meant."[26]

But while Locke's position is helpful, it is marred by his insistence upon consent as the origin and basis of political authority. Perhaps this is a reflection of the extent to which Locke was a prisoner of the genetic models of politics predominant in seventeenth-century thought. In a more specific sense, as we suggested in chapter 4, perhaps his preoccupation with the rejection of Filmer led to the simple exchange of one genetic model for another. In any case, Locke presents two distinct theories of political obligation, a set of consent theories designed to account for political authority and the origin of private property and a trust theory designed to evaluate ongoing governments with a view toward judging the right to revolt. There is no logical connection, nor does

Locke attempt to offer one, between chapters 1 to 9 and the rest of the *Second Treatise*.

Yet Locke has unquestionably given us a valuable starting point, and what we need to do now is to examine these meanings of trust in more detail, unburdened by a second model of political obligation. We need to ask what it means to trust someone, how trust comes about, and whether there are identifiable validating conditions of trust. All of these questions are questions about the structure of trust. And since trust, as with a whole family of words, attempts to provide a link between what men say and what they feel or think or believe or even do, the question "What does it mean to trust someone?" (and questions about the whole structural apparatus of trust) can be answered through an analysis of its grammar.

We might begin by considering a simple example. Smith, Jones's neighbor, takes Jones's television set in order to repair it. Jones, unaware of Smith's kindness, is concerned when he comes home and finds his set missing. Now according to consent theory, it is clear that Smith had no right to fix the set. We might imagine various circumstances, such as Jones nodding his head the night before when Smith thought he knew what was wrong with the television, which we might wish to construe as evidence of consent on Jones's part, but without some sign of permission we are unable to provide a moral evaluation of Smith and Jones's relationship within the context of consent theory. Yet there may be extenuating factors which might lead the owner to hesitate asserting his right over the set, and they may be irrelevant to the presence of consent. Jones, the owner of the set, may have said, "Next time let me know that you're taking my set" or simply "Thanks a lot for fixing my set." Yet Jones's mild rebuke or even his appreciation to Smith could have brought other responses. If a stranger came to the door and said "I've heard your T.V. set needs fixing; let me do it," Jones would hardly give permission nor would he sit comfortably if he found a note to that effect when he came home in the evening. Similarly, if he found out that six-year-old Jimmy Smith had taken the television to repair it, we might expect a different reaction. The point of all this is that Jones's failure to rebuke the repairman for not asking permission results from some interceding relationship between the two men. Smith might have said, "I was hesitant about taking your TV when you weren't there," and Jones might have responded, "Don't be silly, I trust you." There is something about Smith that allows Jones to waive a specific transfer of rights to his property. Much of the same reaction occurs when one is offered a receipt or a contract or a promise from another. The offer is passed off as inappropriate. Jones trusts Smith. In fact, he may not even say "I trust you" but only wave his hand away or say that is not necessary. He may even be mildly insulted at an offer to formalize a transaction.

What is meant then when one says "I trust you" or acts on the basis of trust? Moreover, how does one become trustworthy? In the above case, at least, it is fairly clear what Jones means when he says he trusts Smith. He trusts Smith will not sell his television; that is, he believes Smith when he tells him he took the set to fix it, and he believes Smith can fix the set or at least has a reasonable chance of fixing the set. When Jones tells Smith, "Don't be silly, I trust you," he is saying "I trust (that you will do what you say)" and "I trust in your ability and judgment." When a person trusts another he has a notion of what that other person will do and is quite willing to frame his actions upon this assessment. When he trusts another he may also be doing more than implicitly predicting an action, he may be accepting another's judgment or view of the situation. When Jones trusted Smith to fix his television, he was, beyond believing that Smith actually intended to repair it, also relying upon Smith to fix it. If he had put his attitude into words he might have said, "I accept Smith's evaluation of the set's condition." That is, if Jones himself knew about television sets and how to repair them, he thinks he would come to the same conclusion about its state of repair that Smith now holds. When someone says "trust me, you look fine" and we don't then change our tie or jacket, we have concluded that if we were in the position of the assessor we would arrive at the same conclusion about our own attire or appearance. Trust here involves the acceptance of another's opinion as our own. This notion of trust as reliance arises in situations in which we do not feel we are in a position to judge or act. In the case of the television set it is the fact that we do not have the expertise; in the case of the assessment of our appearance, it is because we are not certain of our impartiality, or because we simply do not know exactly what to do. Should, however, Jones's set lose its picture or never be seen again or should we arrive at a party improperly dressed, we are faced with the task of reevaluating our friends and reassessing our anticipation of what another will do or who can be relied upon. The next time we might try to fix our own set or we might treat Smith differently or we may go by our own judgment about dress. Trust has its own limits.

When someone says "I trust you" he means that he feels that he can anticipate another's actions (or more precisely, he feels that another means what he says and will do what he says) or that another has some "special characteristic" which deserves his abeyance of judgment. In the first case, one acts as if another's intended future action is a present one. In the second case, since there is no elucidation of what exactly is intended (except the broad intention of acting in another's interest), one acts as if he knew what is supposed to occur. Both instances of trust involve anticipation or prediction. The first prediction is based upon the recipient's stated intention to do something in particular, the second upon the recipient's intention to act in a certain way. While both cases of trust arise from an assessment of the recipient, the latter is based upon a "special characteristic" of the recipient rather than any particular expected response. As such the latter is the more serious action for an agent to take if only because the assessment of performance is more difficult. It is easier to determine whether a recipient of trust did what he said he was going to do than to determine if he acted in our interests. This possible ambiguity over performance creates problems over the contention that trust has its limits. How do we know when a recipient with this "special characteristic" has been worthy of our trust? When we say "I trust in your judgment," precisely what are we getting ourselves into? For that matter, when we employ the other use of trust, when we say "I trust you (to do what you say)" are we restricting ourselves in any way? What we need to ask now that we have a preliminary statement is "In what ways have the status of both parties changed?" It is clear that when we say "I consent" we are doing something. We are transferring moral rights in a particular sort of way. When we say "I trust you" or "I trust in your judgment," are we doing the same thing? In short, we must ask, "Is there a relationship between trust and obligation?"

One way in which we might better understand what one is doing or "getting himself into" when he says "I trust you" or "Trust me" is to examine John Austin's distinction between constative and performative utterances.[27] Austin maintained that while it was true that many statements were descriptions — descriptions of actions one was doing or would do — there was a wholly different class of utterances which were not properly speaking descriptions at all. For to issue these utterances was to actually perform an action. Constative utterances were statements such as "the sun rose at six A.M. this morning," "I was born on May 4, 1952," "My dog is a black and white collie." Performative utterances included statements such as "I promise," "I consent," "I declare (war)," "I bet." One of Austin's concerns was to indicate that there were all sorts of utterances which were not statements per se but which nevertheless were not nonsensical. They required their own standards of meaning; exclusively empirical tests of truth and falseness were inapplicable to a determination of sense or nonsense. But the more interesting concern of Austin's, for us at least, was his attempt at placing a large part of our vocabulary of morals into a model of what we might call internal justification and explanation. If when I said "I promise" I was doing something (committing myself to do something), then questions like "Are promises obligatory?" or "Why keep promises?" become tautological. Once the distinction between saying and doing is eliminated, one is asking "Why ought I to do what I ought to do?"[28] We need not accept an Austinian solution to promise-keeping to note that there do appear to be classes of words which in certain contexts and under certain conditions do constitute a performance of an action. In fact, a good deal of the vocabulary of moral discourse (consent, promise, contract, forgive, thank) involves performance of actions. The task of moral philosophy in these cases is to indicate as precisely as possible what conditions and contexts are required for a performance to occur. Austin says as much:

> Beside the uttering of the words of the so-called performative, a good many other things have as a general rule to be right and to go right if we are to be said to have happily brought off our action. What these are we may hope to discover by looking at and classifying types of cases in which something goes wrong and the act — marrying, betting, bequeathing, and christening, or what not is therefore at least to some extent a failure.[29]

Austin offered six conditions for performatives. When things "went wrong" with a performative utterance (when one of the conditions was absent) , Austin called the performative "infelicitous."[30]

Austin's work has been mentioned because we shall find that it can be a critical aid to us in our analysis of trust. We cannot, strictly speaking, classify types of cases in which things go wrong with the act of trust. We make this claim with some trepidation, but not with resignation or sadness. Most theories of obligation make use of some performative (promising, consenting, contracting, thanking, or expressing gratitude) and proceed to determine if, in any particular political system or in any particular situation, anything has "gone wrong" with the action in question.

It is clear that when I say "I do" in a marriage ceremony, I am placing myself under far different obligations than when I say "I do" in my room in front of a mirror. Similarly, if I sprinkled water on my brother's head while saying "I baptize you in the name of . . ." the act has a far different meaning than if a minister performed it. Two of the actions are performatives, the others are, at most, bogus or "infelicitous" performatives. They carry no obligations and they have no meaning (at least in terms of actual performance — in the first I was practicing, in the second I was joking). More difficult cases arise when my speech act is not totally unrelated to a performative but on the other hand is not, strictly speaking, an explicit performative. For instance, I say to an acquaintance, "I'll see you tomorrow morning." The next morning, I am not at the place I said I was going to be. I may have overslept or forgotten what I said or even had a more pressing engagement. I see my friend that afternoon and he is a bit annoyed, if not downright angry. He says, "You promised to meet me this morning." I reply that I said nothing of the kind — all I said was that I would see you tomorrow morning. My friend contends, "By saying you would see me you were saying 'I promise to see you.'" I answer by saying, "I didn't see myself as promising anything, I was only saying what I intended to do tomorrow morning. If I had promised to be there, I would have been there. In any case, I would not have promised to meet you without thinking it over and deciding if I could make it."[31]

The argument of the implicit performative (by saying X, you were saying Y) is the sort of argument which a performative theory of political obligation is always forced to fall back upon. Once a theorist insists that only consent can account for political obligation, he assumes the burden of establishing when consent actually occurs. It is no problem (on these terms) to speak of consent at the institution of a new political system, but there is a problem when one looks for a performative capable of explaining political obligation in an ongoing political system. Without exception, consent theorists are forced into an implicit theory of political obligation by devising

concepts like tacit or indirect or hypothetical consent.[32]
The citizen must ask "In saying X, was I saying Y?"
in order to determine his obligation to the state. In actual
political systems, it is the state which determines (it
does not ask) whether a citizen "in saying X, was saying
Y." The determination of the validity (or on Austin's
terms, the "felicity") of a speech act is clearly out of
the hands of the agent.

The fact that the determination of a performative may,
in certain contexts, be out of control of the agent occurred
to Austin and ultimately led him to abandon his per-
formative-constative distinction for a more general theory
of speech acts.[33] It will be helpful for us to briefly list
them in the hope that they may tell us something about
the relationship between trust and obligation:

1. Verdictives: "[They] consist in the delivering of
a finding, official or unofficial, upon evidence or
reasons as to value or fact. . . . Verdictives have
obvious connections with truth and falsity as regards
soundness and unsoundness or fairness and un-
fairness." Examples are: acquit, convict, rule,
diagnose, reckon, find (as a matter of fact).

2. Exercitives: "An exercitive is the giving of a
decision in favour of or against a certain course of
action, or advocacy of it. It is a decision that
something is to be so, as distinct from a judgment
it is so: it is advocacy that it should be so, as opposed
to an estimate that it is so. . . . Its consequences
may be that others are 'compelled' or 'allowed' or
'not allowed' to do certain acts." Examples of exercitives are: appoint, degrade, command, levy, choose,
plead, press, entreat, vote for, claim.

3. Commissives: "[They] are typified by promising or

otherwise undertaking; they commit you to doing something." . . . Examples are: promise, contract, convenant, consent, vow, swear, declare for.

4. Behabitives: "Behabitives include the notion of reaction to other people's behavior and fortunes and of attitudes and expressions of attitudes to someone else's past conduct or imminent conduct. There are obvious connections with both stating or describing what our feelings are and expressing, in the sense of venting our feelings, though behabitives are distinct from both of these." Examples are: protest, dare, thank sympathize, drink to, don't mind, bid you farewell.

5. Expositives: "Expositives are used in acts of exposition involving the expounding of views, the conduting of argument, and the clarifying of usages and of references." Examples are: state, affirm, deny, emphasize, illustrate, answer.[34]

Many of the above descriptions are pregnant with possibilities for political philosophy. For instance, Austin's inclusion of "vote for" as an exercitive rather than as a commissive is far from the position taken by most consent theorists. But we cannot afford the luxury of exploring these at this time. However, we would like to consider the possibilities of locating the word "trust" (in "I trust you" or "Trust me") within Austin's broader classification. Clearly, trust is not a verdictive. It is not only "infelicitous" but nonsensical for a judge or arbitrator or a jury to say "Trust me" to a contestant in a suit or to say "Trust me" as he would say "We find you guilty of . . ." or "We rule. . . ." Trust as a speech act ("Trust me!") cannot be ordered up by virtue of the speaker's official position. While a jury's conviction makes a felon or an umpire's "ball four!" makes a walk, neither can dictate trust. Both parties are judges or umpires in a situation of trust. This is an important point and we shall return to it in a moment.

The concept of trust is not entirely inconsistent with the exercitive. One can think of contests in which trust is employed as advocacy. We frequently say "He cannot be trusted" or "You can trust him" as a piece of advice. It is less clear that the consequences of using trust in this manner "compel" or "allow" others to do certain acts in the way in which "appoint" or "choose" do. If Jones acts on the basis of Smith's advice that Brown "can be trusted" and Brown violates that trust, Jones might complain to Smith. Certainly Smith might be compelled to justify his advice or explain where it went wrong. He could say, for instance, that he had always found Brown to be reliable. The complaint might eventually lead to a discussion of whether Smith himself was trustworthy. Smith does have an obligation to tell the truth. But when we are adding requirements to the exercitive which Austin may not have intended. An argument could possibly be made that trust is a weak exercitive; more likely than not, however, we would conclude that trust is irrelevant to those speech acts Austin calls exercitives.

The commissive is what remains of Austin's performative. Our central question here is whether trust as a speech act commits one to do something in the way in which promising, consenting, or contracting do. This is a crucial question since we are asking "how does trusting oblige?" We will look at both the rule anticipation or rule reliability and "special characteristic" use of trust we discussed earlier. We must be careful to note that both parties (the recipient of trust and the agent) may both assume obligations. Jones says to Smith, "I trust you." How, if at all, has the relationship between Jones and Smith been altered? Is Jones now obligated to accept Smith's judgment? Suppose Jones changes his mind and decides to pick out his girlfriend's birthday present himself or have his television fixed at a store or asks for a receipt for goods exchanged. There may be innumerable reasons for Jones's withdrawal from his arrangements with Smith. Yet there are five obvious ones which are particularly important to our discussion:

1. Jones can conclude that he does not believe what Smith says (he will do).

2. Jones can deny that Smith possesses the special characteristics required for trust.

3. Jones contends that while he "trusts" Smith in the sense indicated in 1, the possibility of some unanticipated intervening event may place him in a disastrously vulnerable position.

4. Jones contends that the matter at hand is simply "too important" to depend upon a special characteristic trust relationship with Smith.

5. Jones contends that, while he trusts Smith in both senses of 1 and 2, he feels he must operate independently of Smith's expertise or aid.

The first two instances above are most serious. To tell another than you cannot, in full confidence, frame your actions upon his stated intentions is coming quite close to denying his worth as a moral agent. The denial in 2 is not quite as serious although it is no less damaging to future social relationships. For one to question another's moral or technical judgment, once that judgment is acknowledged, is to significantly alter the status of both

agents. This "equalization," or more properly, "reequa-
lization'" of roles is done at the expense of one agent.
To say that one can no longer trust another to act in
one's interests or to do the right thing will not be taken
lightly by the other party. Expertise, moral or technical,
is not casually relinquished once it has been acknowledged
Nevertheless, the denial of the special characteristic
rule of trust still leaves the onetime recipient with
a status equal to the agent. It is possible for one to refuse
to trust another's alleged expertise but still be willing to
trust him in the other sense (that is, in predicting his
actions) .

We must conclude, then, that an agent who denies
a recipient either the rule-reliance or special characteristic notion of trust undertakes a serious (and delicate)
task.

This task, however, does not involve the seriousness
which accompanies breaking a promise or even withdrawing consent. In the former, the promiser must justify
a discrepancy between his stated intentions and his actions. The recipient of a promise has depended upon
him to follow through his intentions. In a trust relationship, it is the agent who "Does the relying." The roles
have been switched and it behooves us to take account
of this when we are trying to determine the seriousness
of withdrawing trust. This is not to say that an agent's
withdrawal of trust can be capricious or even casual.
The agent must consider the impact of the denial upon
the recipient and he must assess the recipient's response
in any future relationship. But this is a requirement of
all social relations. It is not unique to trust nor to doing
one's duty in general. In any case there is an internal
constraint involved. An agent who withdraws his trust
or refuses to offer it is necessarily committing himself

to "go it alone" in his choices and actions. He must act without help, without the advantage of predictability. Men rarely willingly choose to operate in a world devoid of certainty or at least of probabilities, relying on nothing save the knowledge of their own judgments.

While an agent certainly assumes a new role toward the recipient of his trust, we could hardly contend that specific obligations are attached to this role. We cannot say "You are obligated to trust me" or "It is your duty to trust me" without trading on the ordinary use of the term. This is not to say that a refusal to trust another cannot be characterized as "unreasonable" or "unjustifiable" or generally "illconceived" or mistaken. Nor does it mean that pleas for trust and their acceptance or rejection are questions which lie beyond serious dialogue. Philosophy (including political philosophy) does not leave men to choose courses of action indiscriminately when moral obligations are not in question.

The position on the standard regarding the withdrawal of trust just outlined is of considerable importance in relation to the issue of liberal dilemma which we have chosen to focus upon in our discussion of political obligation. Liberals have not been entirely certain about what personality attributes are most desirable for citizens in a liberal state. Some of this reticence is due to the liberal belief in the importance of the development of the nonpolitical aspect of people's lives. But much of it relates to the liberal difficulty with the concept of political obligation itself.

Bentham suggests the image of a man busily concerned with his own matters, occasionally lifting up his eyes to the political situation to coldly calculate the mischiefs of resistance against the mischiefs of obedience. Hobbes's citizen looks up more often and perhaps not quite so dispassionately. Smith laments the propensity of the citizen to magnify problems close to his own interests and for that reason seems to prefer political quiescence. Jefferson applauds the farmer patriot who would pick up a shovel at the least governmental provocation. Locke suggests much the same image but clearly is a bit relieved to observe that revolt is likely to occur only after a long train of abuses.

But all of these views of the liberal citizenry are cast in the model of a presumed moral duty of obedience, however it is conceived and however narrowly or widely each writer prefers to circumscribe it. The advantage of the concept of trust as a model for evaluating the relationship between citizen and state is the very absence of any moral duty to obey. While moral duties are appropriate to those who undertake political authority, the requirement of citizenship can best be described as one of "judiciousness." The state is justified in expecting sound judgment, prudence, discreetness, and sensibility from the citizenry. It is not entitled to require anything more.

What of the remaining cases in which trust is rejected? The first, the case in which Jones appears to be willing to accept the anticipation of Smith's actions, is based upon a realization of the contingency of all human actions. Jones is willing to trust *Smith*. However, he does not feel he can anticipate the range of possibilities which may interfere with Smith's intentions. He may trust Smith with his property without a lease but he may not trust Smith's wife if something should happen to Smith. Or he may not be able to anticipate what the state will do with his property in Smith's absence. In short, an agent may frequently find that the trustworthiness of a recipient will not by itself be sufficient to deliver

a trust relationship. The recipient himself may die or
go insane, and Jones does not feel he can anticipate what
those who will be in a position to interpret Smith's words
will do. Jones's willingness to trust others may, in fact,
be dependent upon the entire social milieu in which he
operates. He may be surrounded by any number of
trustworthy men but he may not avail himself of any
of them if he cannot anticipate the course of actions
should any of these men be absent. But we are getting
a bit ahead of ourselves here since the relation between
trust and social structure must await examination later
in this essay. Suffice it to say that the argument offered
here is a much broader one than that involved in a
sociology of trust. It says that the anticipation of another's
action is always fraught with some uncertainty even if
this uncertainty is linked to human mortality. We may
trust that another will help us in some impending
emergency. Obviously, the recipient of this trust cannot
help us if he is dead or incapacitated. While this is not
a calculation which most of us make when we trust others,
it is a calculation, however, which we must make when
the actions we trust others to do are of such significance
that their failure may be disastrous to the agent. This
is certainly one reason why wills are drawn up, deeds
are kept in safe deposit boxes, and indeed promises are
extracted.[35] It is not that the recipients themselves cannot
be expected to do what they say, but that the transactions
involved demand an assurance which trust simply cannot
guarantee.

In the last case the meaning of importance changes
a bit. An agent does not reject reliance upon others
because of possible unanticipated events independent of
a recipient's intentions. He refuses to accept or continue
accepting the judgment of others because he feels certain

matters should be carried through by himself. The reasons for such a decision can, of course, vary. An agent may decline the trust of others because he feels that only a decision reached by himself will develop his capacities for judgment. Frequently, a parent or a friend will say, "'Let me take care of this for you." One answers that while he respects his friend's judgment (that is, that his friend's decision will indeed reflect his interests) or is confident that the object in question will be taken care of, this is an action best undertaken by himself. He may respond by saying that "it's not that I don't trust you, but if I don't make these arrangements myself I'll never be able to fend for myself." When the offer of trust interferes with an individual's capacity to act, it is not "imprudent," "unreasonable," or "ill-conceived" for it to be rejected. This is not an unimportant point because it emphasizes two more basic limitations upon the concept of trust. It suggests that trust relationships may be undesirable for an agent in certain situations, and it suggests that an assessment of the efficiency of performance within and without a trust relationship may be inapplicable to the justifiability of the rejection of trust. The latter point may need some comment. In the case we are discussing, it is not a relevant argument for a potential recipient of trust to contend that he could complete an action more efficiently or make a better decision than the agent. For the agent has claimed that he needs to make this decision himself for precisely the same reasons. The "special characteristic" basis for trust is what the agent hopes to eliminate by undertaking this and other decisions on his own.

What we have seen in examining cases in which trust is rejected is that it becomes extremely difficult for us to fit the agent in a trust relationship into the requirements for a performative. Particularly in the last three cases we find that trust (either as anticipation or reliance) cannot be demanded in the way in which performance of a promise or contract can be demanded. Trust is not "broken" by the agent. It may be rejected unwisely or unreasonably but these terms are not the stuff from which obligations or duties are made.

But does trust oblige the recipient? I think we will find that "being trusted" (as distinct from "being trustworthy") clearly involves obligations. How a recipient becomes obliged, however, differs considerably from the way we normally consider that obligations work. If we continue our examination of the structure of trust we will see that a recipient is under two broad, related sets of obligations. One includes those duties which any moral actor holds. The other includes those obligations which specifically arise from becoming a recipient of trust. Let me illustrate. Two students are taking an examination. The professor leaves the room. Student A asks student B for the answer to a question on the examination. Student B refuses. His reasons for refusal can take either (or both) of two forms. He can say, "I won't give you an answer because cheating is wrong," or he can say, "I won't give you an answer because the professor has trusted us (to work independently)." The latter response does not mean that B would be willing to cheat if the professor had a proctor watch the students when he left the room — that is, if the professor had not trusted his students. It does, however, place the reason for B's actions in a different context. B has said in effect that he accepts another's anticipation of his actions as binding upon his own behavior. Here the professor's action (his trust of his students) has emphasized or made explicit the students' roles as moral actors.

Being trusted by another can make the resort to purely egoistic motives more difficult to justify. Certainly cheating or lying is morally wrong, but when someone denies a self-interested course of action by saying "I can't do that, he trusts me," he has eliminated that area of human action which we all choose too often. This is the area of doing right when we are not called upon to do so. Being trusted makes supererogatory acts obliging. It is one thing for a man to recognize a duty and to do what he says he will do; it is quite another to recognize that others explicitly depend upon his consistency between intention and deed. We cannot disregard an injunction to do what we say or to tell the truth by contending "I never asked him to trust me," but we certainly can as recipients of reliance break a trust as surely as promises and contracts are broken.

The treatment of political obligation in terms of trust provides us with the only accommodation which the fundamental irreconcilability between the exercise of moral judgment and the exercise of political authority allows. The rule-anticipation feature of trust provides a framework for a rational evaluation of political structure. If a citizen is unable to anticipate the actions of his rulers, he is denied a capacity for moral evaluation of the state. Without knowing what the state will do next, he is unable to justify the exercise of political authority and he is unable to question or assess the direction, much less the worth, of state policy.[36] The existence of Locke's "stated promulgated rules" makes moral discourse with the state possible even if it ultimately fails. Many theories of political obligation have recognized the necessity of known and ordered rules for society; the fault lies in confusing the citizen's need for such rules with his acceptance of the rules themselves. In other words, performative theories have mistaken rule anticipation for rule acceptance as a basis for political obligation.

The other feature of trust, special characteristic reliance, allows for the exercise of political authority. It has an advantage over consent accounts of political obligation in that it involves the abeyance rather than the surrender of moral judgment. The citizen accepts the judgment of the ruler as his own to the extent to which he believes the ruler as recipient of his trust acts as he would were he in his position. This special characteristic reliance is not a rule-governed anticipation but it is an anticipation that the ruler will act in a manner consistent with the way in which the citizen as agent thinks he is supposed to act. This, of course, means that the ruler must justify this special characteristic which allows for his actions. Special characteristics justification can vary from an argument which adheres as a trait in the recipient himself (such as his wisdom in past situations) to the way in which he arrived at his position (such as recognition by others in an election). In other words, he may say "trust me (to do the right thing)" because I have done the right thing in the past or because I have certain credentials to make the correct judgment or because others have recognized my abilities and you should consider the judgment of others. The agent is now in a position to assess his alleged wisdom or credentials or to decide if the judgment of others is important enough to allow him to anticipate the correctness of some impending decision. The argument for special characteristics may also be quite fundamental. The ruler may say, "Trust me, I am the only person in a position to make such a decision — this is the nature of political authority." In this case, the agent has the recourse of rejecting political authority (or at least of rejecting political authority as it is presently constituted). As we have seen, consent theory does recognize the logical necessity of political authority curtailing individual judgment. It proceeds, however, to justify that curtailment by looking for instances of individual relinquishment. The benefit of the concept of trust lies in its emphasis upon the agent's *current assessment* of the state as a basis of political obligation. If that assessment is one of trust, the citizen has afforded the ruler with the opportunity to act and with the duty of justifying his ongoing performance. As we have noted in our earlier section, the offer of trust can be rejected for a number of reasons. It can also be rejected at a point in time after the special characteristic was once recognized. New insights and new conditions can change one man's evaluation of another. As an explanation of our duties, consent can become a moral Frankenstein; trust never allows for its creation.

It is time for us to set out precisely what sort of answer we have developed to the question "Why should I obey the state?" At the risk of oversimplification, our answer up to this point is something like this. One ought to obey the state to the extent to which he trusts those in political authority.[37] By trust we mean that relationship between agent and recipient in which the former relies upon the latter's actions or judgment. That reliance is based upon an anticipation of the recipient's actions. This anticipation may result from the belief that known prescribed rules govern the behavior of the recipient or it may result from the belief that the recipient holds some "special characteristic" which deserves departure from any particular rule-governed response. The agent may withdraw his trust from the recipient at any time during the actions or judgments in question. In doing so, he must base his refusal upon a denial of the two sorts of anticipation mentioned above or upon an argument from the ultimate contingency of any anticipated action, or upon an argument from "self-development." Those in authority, the recipients of trust, hold obligations to the citizen as agent to fulfill the expectations of trust.[38]

Relations between citizen and state are certainly possible without trust but political authority cannot be justified without it. Certainly the state will go on acting as if it is trusted when a citizen or citizens no longer recognize it as recipient. Take, for example, a familiar late-show dialogue between a blackmailer and his victim. The extortionist demands a sum of money in return for some incriminating pictures. The victim, anxious to make this his first and last payment, asks, "How can I trust you (to destroy the negatives)?" The pathetic nature of the appeal for trust under these conditions is brought home by the villain's sneering response, "You have no choice, do you?" If the victim does eventually make payment, this does not mean, of course, that he has really decided to trust the extortionist. In fact, he cannot reasonably foresee the blackmailer acting consistent with his stated intentions. Given previous examples of the blackmailer's actions and the nature of his activity itself, the victim is likely to expect future actions to be other than what he is told they will be. Nor does the blackmailer possess any special characteristics which would allow the agent to anticipate actions apart from rule anticipation. Yet because of the unfavorable circumstances governing this particular relationship, the agent is "obliged" *to act as if* the extortionist will perform according to the rules he has ostensibly created.[39]

This example suggests, among other things, that we

cannot talk meaningfully about trust by referring solely to performance of actions by virtue of appealing to and accepting rules or special characteristics. Relationships of trust must be performed under circumstances conducive to interdependence; neither party can possess a monopoly of mutually coveted resources. Recently a number of theorists have attempted to incorporate the notion of rule anticipation and subsequent rule governed behavior into theories of political obligation.[40] But by failing to distinguish the existence and justification of social rules from the reasons for which they are followed, they have identified obligation claims from the viewpoint of the obligation claimant. This is the error that H. L. A. Hart has committed in his *Concept of Law*.[41] On his account an individual is obliged to the extent to which his activities fall under a social rule. Such rules are determined by the extent to which they are considered important to the maintenance of social life and as such are accompanied by more or less strong sanctions. Hart is very much concerned with distinguishing authority from coercion and does so by accounting for obligations in terms of rule-governed behavior. What he fails to recognize is the inequality of individuals in society and in relation to the state. Social rules clearly benefit some and exploit others. Hart maintains that at least some members of society regard certain social rules as a general standard to be followed by all. It is this internal aspect of social rules and Hart's ambiguity as to who actually must recognize a rule for it to be obligatory that raises the specter of status bias which we associated with our accounts of current conceptions of conscience and performative theories of obligation. It does not require a great flight of imagination to envision a rule-governed society that systematically deprives a particular group from rights enjoyed by others on the grounds that such a rule is necessary for the maintenance of society. This is the sort of argument uniformly advanced by those objecting to the abolition of slavery, extension of suffrage, penal reform, and a score of other attempts at reformulating the basic social rules. In order to speak of social rules as a basis for political obligation we need to consider their relation to trust. Just as the victim has no obligation to the blackmailer, individuals or groups in society have no obligation to those who, when asked to give evidence of their intentions, say in effect, "You have no choice, do you?" Certain social conditions are necessary to meet the requirements of trust; status advantages must be ameliorated to accommodate the demands of society-wide rule performance. When such conditions are not met, an explanation of ongoing rules no longer provides an adequate justification for trust.

If the relative equality of social class is a possible requisite for a relation of trust between citizen and state, there are certain practices of the liberal democratic state which *may*, in addition, provide for civic trust. These practices roughly correspond to the conditions requisite to the structure of trust outlined in the last section of this chapter. The constitutional state provides for a system of relatively fixed rules which the citizen can rely upon and measure against ongoing state policy. Elections can at least provide for patterned leadership succession. But they can also present one sort of argument for the special characteristic aspect of trust. The office holder makes the ongoing decision of state and as such creates new social rules (within the framework of a constitution it is to be hoped). In this context, the citizen can only anticipate that his representative will act in his interests. Similarly, the principle of majority rule in the election of officials of state and in the decisions of governing bodies may correspond to trust to the extent that they foster interdependence of groups or individuals or at least discourage a monopoly of political or economic resources in society. At some point in time, however, the recipient of trust must justify that reliance. In this sense, elections may serve as mechanisms for the retrieval of trust.

We have also noted the conditions under which trust can be denied or rejected. The liberal democratic state attempts to account for the rejection of trust according to the contingency and importance rules by its insistence upon the explicit guarantee of civil liberties. If some areas of action are simply too important to be left to the decision of those who happen to be managing the state, certainly among them are the principles historically demanded by liberals: due process, freedom of speech, assembly and petition, freedom from unreasonable search and seizure, and involuntary servitude Similarly, the argument for the citizen's direct administration of state, even at the risk of alleged more efficient performance when managed by others, corresponds to the self-development principle discussed earlier.

But it must be emphasized that these rules of correspondence between the concept of trust and practices of the liberal democratic state are offered with the utmost caution. The movement from the structure of trust to political institutions is fraught with all sorts of difficulties. Let me mention only one as an example. An official of state seeks compliance to a law or the legal system in general. He presents his case to the citizen much in the same way in which one says to his neighbor, "Trust me, you look fine." The citizen responds by asking "What special characteristic can you claim that would convince me to trust you will act in my interests?" The official answers by saying that a majority of the people have elected him (or reelected him) and that a majority of the people comply with the legal system. This argument, however, equates rule compliance with trust. There may be all sorts of reasons for general compliance with the legal system, none of which are relevant to the dissenter if they are not based upon trust. Moreover, these rules of correspondence are no guarantee of actual compliance with the structure of trust.

Perhaps another way in which we might assess the virtues of trust as an account of the relation between citizen and state in liberal democratic regimes is to present a discussion of the practice of civil disobedience. During the past decade enormous attention has been paid to this phenomenon. There is no doubt that the legion of books and articles devoted to it was a reaction to the turmoil of the 1960's. As a result, sympathizers and skeptics may have grossly exaggerated its overall significance for society. Discussions of civil disobedience now have a certain staleness about them. Few any longer contend that civil disobedience represents a modern addition to constitutional theory or that it looses "dark forces" lying "quiescent beneath the surface of our national life."[42] But a case can be made that the most fruitful clarification of political problems occurs in an atmosphere of quiet and perhaps even in mild resignation. No less important is the fact that the questions raised by civil disobedience are perennial ones.

It we look at those who struggled with this problem in recent years, we detect a basic problem in the advocacy of civil disobedience. The classic question raised in any account along these lines is "What characteristics must be present for an action to deserve the title civil disobedience?" If the law is broken in certain specified ways, is it qualitatively distinct from ordinary criminal activity or revolution? Certainly part of the trouble involved in dealing with this question comes from the fact that models of civil disobedience have been derived in large part from those who have not held liberal-democratic aims. Thoreau passed off voting as moral gaming and Gandhi described his politics as one of "enlightened anarchy."[43] But the problems do go deeper than historical reference. They derive from the broader theory of political obligation that is shared by civil disobedience advocates. On the one hand, if one posits a system in which he owes a moral duty to obey the state, he has considerable difficulty in justifying resistance to that system. The problem is much like what Herbert Storing has described when he says that the civil disobedient's claim to fealty to the law is comparable to one who tries to demonstrate his respect for womanhood by allowing himself to be slapped by a woman he has just hit.[44] The tendency is to add restriction after restriction to his account of civil disobedience until one wonders how meaningful such an action will be. On the other hand, if one posits a state from which one is radically alienated, he has as much difficulty justifying respect to that system. Thus for Howard Zinn to "accept jail penitently . . . is to switch suddenly to a spirit of subservience, to demean the seriousness of protest."[45]

The best way in which we can illustrate this paradox is to consider an example from each position. Then we will have a perspective from which to see how our account of political obligation can avoid these difficulties.

There are numerous examples that we might use to discuss the first position. It is stated most clearly and carried furthest by John Rawls in his *A Theory of Justice*.[46] Rawls's book is huge and complex but the point which we shall use for illustration is a simple one and does not slight recognition of his larger effort. Rawls attempts to derive a set of principles for a just society from an account of what we would want in an "original position" of ignorance of our wealth, intelligence, and skills. A society which fully incorporates these principles into practice deserves our obedience on the basis of our "'natural duty" to support just institutions. Rawls further contends that since there is no way to characterize a feasible procedure to lead to just legislation, the citizen may find himself obligated to obey unjust laws. Majorities "are found to make mistakes"; our duty is to uphold the just institutions from which some unjust laws may emanate. Rawls believes that in the long run the burden of injustice will be "more or less evenly distributed over different groups in society."

The problem of civil disobedience arises in a "nearly just" society, one in which there exists a "viable constitutional regime more or less satisfying the principles of justice" and a "relatively well-ordered, although not perfectly ordered," social system. Here we find a conflict of duties much more sharp. Some resolution is required. Rawls asks: "At what point does the duty to comply with laws enacted by a legislative majority . . . cease to be binding in view of the right to defend one's liberties and the duty to oppose injustice?" He regards civil disobedience as a "crucial test case for any theory of the moral basis of society." And he is so enamored of the effects of civil disobedience that in his state creators of a just political system would set up conditions defining civil disobedience as a "morally correct way of maintaining a constitutional regime." Civil disobedience, then, is a morally appropriate way to oppose a regime which one is morally obligated to accept. This is a paradoxical statement, and Rawls attempts to rescue its sense by arguing that although "for the most part the principles of justice are publicly recognized as the fundamental terms of willing cooperation among free and equal persons," civil disobedients are serving "fair notice that in one's sincere and considered opinion the conditions of free cooperation are being violated." Civil disobedience, then, is a delicate act, one in which the agent momentarily stands aside from a moral obligation he still recognizes. It is much like requesting proof of love from a friend. Therefore it can be very informative for us to look at the conditions Rawls feels are necessary for potential civil disobedients to recognize. Civil disobedience must be:

1. a public act comparable to a "public speech."

2. nonviolent because that is consistent with the act as a "mode of address" and because it expresses "disobedience to law within the limits of fidelity to law."

3. resorted to only after legal means of redress have been exhausted.

4. limited to "instances of substantial and clear injustice."

5. postponed if the consequence of other equally oppressed groups doing so as well would lead to the collapse of society.

6. subjected to maxims of prudence. "We may be acting within our rights but nevertheless unwisely if our conduct only serves to provoke the harsh retaliation of the majority."

If we grant that conditions 1–3 are typically accepted by a majority of civil disobedients, we may set them aside, at least for the moment. Condition 4 for Rawls is quite limiting. Civil disobedience can be used in support of eliminating "serious infringements" of the principle of equal liberty and "blatant violations" of the principle of fair equality of opportunity. But even here Rawls has drawn the net around compliance very widely. While it is true that denial of the right to vote (one of Rawls's examples of "serious infringement") is an injustice obvious to all, any informed student of politics would recognize that most forms of oppression are countenanced by such a wide variety of supporting conditions that they are not "obvious to all." In one sense, this is what makes them so serious. Thus, for instance, the refusal to allocate enough voting booths in certain sections of a city seems a petty annoyance, one not serious enough to warrant civil disobedience. But when such a policy creates long lines and discourages groups of people from voting, its consequences can be as great as if there were a constitutional quota on voting rights for certain groups of the population. Similarly, the failure of the government to pick up garbage frequently or regularly appears to be a minor inconvenience. But when this is connected with the fact that there are not enough traffic lights in a district nor enough policemen, together they indicate an uneven distribution of collective goods and a case of injustice.

When we look at Rawls's argument for refusing to support civil disobedience as a remedy for distribution of income (another of Rawls's principles of justice) we can begin to appreciate his dilemma. Here caution is the theme:

Infractions of the difference principle are more difficult to ascertain. There is usually a wide range of conflicting yet rational opinion as to whether this principle is satisfied. The reason for this is that it applies primarily to economic and social institutions and policies. A choice among these depends upon theoretical and speculative beliefs as well as upon a wealth of statistical and other information, all of this seasoned with shrewed judgment and plain hunch. In view of the complexities of these questions, it is difficult to check the influence of self-interest and prejudice, and even if we can do this in our own case, it is another matter to convince others of our good faith (p. 372).

Rawls suggests that tax laws, unless they clearly violate equal liberty, "should not normally be protested by civil disobedience." We are told that the appeal to the sense of justice is "not sufficiently clear." But surely we can imagine scores of economic policies which are patently unfair. But lowering of pay scales, regressive and/or exorbitant taxation and punitive docking of wages are common enough practices in history, and in a "nearly just" society victims should have no trouble pricking the public's conception of justice.

Rawls's reticence in this area can be appreciated if we briefly note his other restrictions. Under condition 5, victimized groups must be aware that there is a limit to which civil disobedience can be engaged in without leading to a breakdown of law and order, "thereby setting in motion consequences unfortunate for all." Since Rawls believes that injured minorities are incapable of judging the relative injustice they have been subjected to, he suggests some rotation or lottery scheme.

Now all these restrictions are puzzling for one who believes at the same time that civil disobedience is so important that it is to be recommended as a morally correct way of maintaining a constitutional regime. One commentator has somewhat wistfully noted that Rawls's conception of civil disobedience can be captured in the slogan, "This hurts me more than it hurts you."[47] The only conclusion we can reach is that Rawls is caught in a rather unpleasant paradox. If the "nearly just" society is really as "well ordered" as Rawls would have us believe, then the resort to civil disobedience would seem to be problematical. A simple declaration that the principles of cooperation may have been violated would cause representatives to scurry to the legislative halls for revaluation. Civil disobedience must not be a "threat"; it must only warn and admonish. Yet if the distinction between warning and threat is to have any significance it becomes blurred by breaking the law publicly. We can think of a thousand ways in which we can admonish others within the bounds of law. If a society is somehow oppressive, Rawls's conception of civil disobedience would appear to be hopelessly restrictive. The citizenry are forced to engage in civil disobedience only when the ruling elite blunders into committing blatant obstructions of justice. In a liberal society where political problems are argued out in the context of acceptance of a plurality of values across continuums like public and private, majority rule and minority right, the ability to continue to conceal and confine issues involving injustice would seem to be limitless. Oppressed minorities would patiently take turns, prudently respecting the possibility of "harsh retaliation" by the majority, appealing their case only to find each becoming mired in liberal casuistry.

Lest this discussion serve to minimize Rawls's effort, let us look at an approach to the problem from a divergent perspective. In a very influential article, Christian Bay has argued that traditional restrictions on civil disobedience are inappropriate to the realities of "what goes on in the name [of democracy] in today's mass societies."[48] Like Rawls, Bay works within a moral model of political obligation (legitimate governments "protect human life and basic human rights") but deals with societies which, in his mind, so use democratic methods to "preserve

the political and socioeconomic *status quo*" that "orderly
political damage has become impracticable."[49] He is therefore anxious to remove certain "myths" associated with
civil disobedience. The sancity of democratically enacted
law perpetuates the status quo:

> Under conditions of democratic pluralism, an uncritical submis-
> sion to the rule of law means not only the shunning of violence
> but also, in effect, the abandonment of all intelligent effort to
> work effectively for changing the system. For it means agreeing
> in advance to live by rules in fact operating to forestall the
> development of democracy in any real sense. These are the rules
> by which the powerful have become more powerful, and the
> powerless more emasculated. . . . Thus the discrepancies between
> our rose-colored perceptions of a government "by the people"
> and the stark realities of poverty and oppression have kept on
> growing.[50]

To further the promotion of a just society, civil
disobedience should be kept apart from "nonviolent action." Instead the doctrine of "carefully chosen and
limited means" to achieve with "maximum economy"
certain ends should take its place. Bay believes that
"for many reasons it seems plausible that such rational
calculation normally will suggest strenuous efforts toward
either avoidance or reduction of violence."[51]

But we are then told that "it will obviously not do,
either, to assert that all laws can be ignored, or that
any particular law can be obeyed or disobeyed as a matter
of convenience."[52] "Nobody in his right mind will support
all disobedience, however, 'civil' regardless of the issues
involved." Some restrictions on civil disobedience are
appropriate, and Bay suggests that they must be "public
and limited." By limited Bay includes the following:[53]

1. Civil disobedience must "fall short of seeking the
complete abolition of the existing legal system."

2. Civil disobedience must fall short of intending the

physical or moral destruction of adversaries, even
if at times a calculable risk of casualties may be
tolerated.

3. Above all, the proclaimed ends of civil disobedience must be formulated with a view to making
them appear morally legitimate to onlookers and to
the public.

Now these restrictions have a certain plausibility about
them but they become (like Rawls's) puzzling when one
measures them against the larger theory and against
the assessment of the society they are designed to improve.

How would one treat the actions of the Danes who
publicly wore the Star of David after the Nazis com-
manded all Jews to display them? Certainly they did
not seek only to reform the Nazi legal structure, nor
were they reticient about intending the moral destruction
of the occupation forces. How does one reconcile the
use of violence with the commitment to avoid the physical
or moral destruction of adversaries? Either the talk of
economy of means is not to be taken seriously or one
is to strike a blow to the head of an opponent with tears
and solemnity. Even the economy criterion in regard
to violence fails to relate meaningfully to the alleged
predatory character of American society. Perhaps Bay
means that civil disobedients ought to be nonviolent
simply because the "state has more guns." Then we
are left to conclude that morally correct behavior to
regimes most likely to employ violence is a more pliant
form of disobedience. Disobedience becomes less "civil"
in regimes that are reluctant to respond with force. But
common sense tells us that a state which withholds its
use of force in the face of disobedience may well have

more redeeming features than one which does not. Or
perhaps Bay means that violence is rarely productive
because of its unpredictability.[54] But if one grants the
assumption that this continued oppression is eminently
predictable (as Bay appears to believe), it is difficult
on these terms to make a distinction between selective
violence and revolution especially since one can place
some restrictions on force even in the latter case. An
economy of means with regard to violence can be employed by both the civil disobedient and the revolutionary.
The difference is that the latter has drawn a more ex-
extreme picture of the situation.

Despite the attempts of Rawls and Bay, an account
of civil disobedience remains unrelated to their conceptions of political obligation. Certainly part of their
difficulties lie in the fragility of models of ethical disputes
when applied to problems of political action. The practice
of civil disobedience attempts to make this connection
and take it into areas that are perhaps least capable
of sustaining the link. But both writers do seem to appreciate the delicacy of such an operation and yet they
still fail. Perhaps the account offered in these pages
can serve to turn the situation around. Unfortunately
the reader must tolerate an annoying brevity on this
point. If the model of moral duty fails to provide an acceptable account of political obligation in relatively
routinized political situations, it is consistent with our
position to question the general efficacy of civil disobedience. If the conditions necessary for trust are
generally lacking in modern liberal-democratic regimes, it
is unlikely that campaigns of civil disobedience can do
a great deal to bring them about. Only to the extent which
they make specious appeals to trust more difficult for
those in political authority to make does civil disobedience
hope to perform much of a service. Civil disobedience

may be of much more use as a way of registering a withdrawal of trust.

There are two sets of questions we need to ask regarding the appropriateness of civil disobedience and the account of political obligation we have outlined: what is the purpose of civil disobedience in the liberal society and is the practice of civil disobedience consistent with the requirement of judiciousness on the part of the citizenry? In order to begin to ask the first question we need to determine the reasons for the acceptance of citizen demands brought forward by civil disobedience. The case of the blackmailer mentioned above can help us illustrate. Suppose a group in society asks for evidence of the intentions of those in authority, and the reply they receive says in effect, "You have no choice but to trust us, do you?" Now the victimized group may very well respond by saying, "We have resources at our disposal as well — we hereby give notice that certain services will be withheld until you can give us a better account of your intentions." Now it may be that those in authority find the withdrawal of services (or should there be no valuable services in the group's control, general disruption) intolerable and accede to the group's demands. While a sharing of power or equalization of economic goods might be the result of the transaction, there is no reason to believe that the ruling group has acted on the basis of a trust relationship. Quite the contrary, and if we can move this time from a political example to a personal one we can illustrate. If in response to the blackmailer who, when you ask if the negatives will be destroyed, says, "You have no choice, do you?" you respond by pointing a gun at him and say, "Yes, I do — hand them over now," it is unlikely that we would call such a standoff a trust relationship. Now Rawls apparently saw the import of this situation when he urged disobedients only to admonish and not to threaten. The latter violated his model of a morally correct transaction. Bay, on the other hand, mistakes the moral justification for seeking a raw power balance with the methods used to achieve it.

If we may continue with our example, we might also conclude that the blackmailer may well mutter to himself, "Next time, I'll be sure to pack a gun!" When ruling groups engage in this type of thinking, the result is that civil disobedience is only a prelude to revolution or repression. To the extent to which challenging groups mistakenly take victories of this sort as cases of forging trust relationships they are doomed. It is imperative then that disobedients be aware of whether their actions have created a moral tension (to use Martin Luther King's words) in the ruling class or only a retreat for reinforcements. More likely than not in the case of creating economic equality it is the latter. This is not to make the same case as Rawls does in a different fashion. Civil disobedients should only be aware that they are operating outside a trust relationship, and then they ought to restrict their behavior to accord with their own personal safety and respect for maintenance of existing constitutional arrangements.[55]

The case for civil disobedience in regard to the withdrawal of trust in terms of special characteristic reliance and the contingency and self-development rules can be made a bit more forcefully. Here the citizenry is employing a tactic to make an essentially negative action. The state can no longer be trusted by virtue of its expertise or it cannot be trusted in certain crucial areas of an individual's life. At this point the concept of judiciousness fits well into the civil disobedient's appreciation of moral nuances. Publicity, nonviolence without direct provocation, and penalty acceptance are as prudent and discreet ways as have been found for a citizen to make known the intensity of his claims against the state. But even here an aggressive action on the part of those in political authority may quickly lead the citizen to question his overall trust of the state. But at least this treatment will provide a consistent account of the tragedy.

The practices of the modern liberal-democratic state have evolved through centuries of bitter struggle. Yet they may simply not be enough to allow a citizen to trust the state. In this case, one must look for new practices which can meet the conditions for political obligation. Indeed, the major fault of modern liberalism and its American pluralistic variant has been its persistent refusal to consider this question. One step in that direction may well involve the abandonment of the belief that a moral ground of political obligation can be found since the liberal imagination itself forbids any such resolution. Countenance of a restricted conception of morality or forays into the nightmarish world of men pursuing raw self-interests have generally been the only result. Since the very term "political obligation" is so closely related to the assumption of a moral duty of political authority, perhaps the liberal would do well to strike it from his vocabulary. New vocabularies, however modestly they appear to contribute to social change, are a prerequisite to the formation of new political institutions.

Beyond that, precious little advice can be given. The courses of action in the absence of trust in the state are at once varied and quite limited. The inability of political philosophy to speak in the face of the barrel of a gun involves a condemnation of the nature of states, not of those who try to make some sense of men's lives within the context of their persistent existence.

Notes

Chapter 1

1. Benedict Spinoza, *The Chief Works of Benedict Spinoza,* trans. R. H. M. Elwes, 2 vols. (New York: Dover, 1951), 2:6.

2. John Stuart Mill made this quote the frontispiece of his *On Liberty,* declaring that "the only author who has preceded me . . . of whom I thought it appropriate to say anything was Humboldt."

3. Jefferson to Dr. Benjamin Rush, *Life and Selected Writings of Thomas Jefferson,* ed. Adrienne Koch and William Peden (New York: Random House, 1944), p. 558.

4. Jeremy Bentham, "Constitutional Code," in *The Works of Jeremy Bentham,* ed. John Bowring, 11 vols. (Edinburgh: William Tait, 1843–59), 9:5.

5. Adam Smith, *The Theory of Moral Sentiments,* in *Smith's Moral and Political Philosophy, ed.* Herbert W. Schneider (New York: Hafner, 1948), pt. 6, sec. 3, p. 251.

6. John Stuart Mill, *Three Essays on Religion* (London: Longmans, 1885), pp. 20-21.

7. David Hume, "Of the Origin of Government," in *Hume's Moral and Political Philosophy,* ed. Henry D. Aiken (Darien, Conn.: Hafner, 1970), p. 31.

8. Adam Smith, *Wealth of Nations,* in *Smith's Moral and Political Philosophy,* bk. 5, sec. 1, p. 421.

9. Thomas Jefferson to John Adams, *Writings,* p. 702.

10. Bruno Bettelheim, *The Informed Heart: Autonomy in a Mass Age* (Glencoe, Ill.: Free Press, 1961), p. 265.

11. Thomas Paine, *The Complete Writings of Thomas Paine,* ed. Philip S. Foner (New York: Citadel Press, 1945), p. 5.

12. John Locke, *Two Treatises of Government,* ed. Peter Laslett, 2 vols. (New York: New American Library, 1965), 2:324.

13. Ibid., 2:311.

14. Ibid., 2:310.

15. Ibid., 2:308.

16. Ibid., 2:394, 401–2.

17. Ibid., 2:377, 390.

18. Ibid., 2:403, 406.

19. David Hume, *A Treatise on Human Nature,* ed. T. H. Green and T. H. Grose, 2 vols. (London: Longmans, Green, 1898), vol. 2, bk. 2, pt. 2, sec. 2, p. 259.

20. Ibid., pp. 260–61.

21. Ibid., p. 262.

22. Ibid., p. 268.

23. Ibid., p. 306.

24. Ibid.

25. Ibid., p. 308.

26. David Hume, "Of the Original Contract," *Essays: Moral, Political, and Literary,* ed. T. H. Green and T. H. Grose (London: Longmans, Green, 1875), p. 455.

27. Ibid.

28. Ibid., p. 462.

29. Hume, "Of the Origin of Government," *Essays,* p. 114.

30. Ibid.

31. Ibid., p. 115.

32. Hume, "Of the First Principles of Government," *Essays,* p. 111.

33. Hume, "Of Passive Obedience," *Essays,* p. 461.

34. Smith, *Theory of Moral Sentiments,* p. 220.

35. Ibid., p. 160.

36. Ibid., p. 310. Sheldon Wolin, in his zeal to show the "middling" bias of liberalism, suggests the impartial spectator is a sum of the opinions of others, reflections derived from observance of social conformities (*Politics and Vision,* Boston: Little, Brown, 1960, p. 344). Actually, reverence for "the man without" occurs in Smith's political application of his moral theories. Nineteenth-century commentators were in fact critical of the grandeur of the "spectator" and the late introduction of his lesser counterpart. See, for instance, Sir Leslie Stephen, *History of English Thought in the Eighteenth Century,* 2 vols. (New York: Harcourt, Brace and World, 1962), 2:52–65.

37. Smith, "Lectures on Justice, Police, Revenue and Arms," *Moral and Political Philosophy* p. 289.

38. Ibid., p. 287.
39. Ibid.
40. Ibid.
41. Ibid., p. 288.
42. Ibid., p. 310.
43. Bentham, *Principles of Morals and Legislation, Works,* 2:1.
44. Bentham, *A Fragment on Government* (Oxford: Oxford University Press, 1891), p. 228.
45. Bentham, "Defense of Usury" *Works,* 5:5.
46. Bentham, *Constitutional Code,* in *Works,* 5–7.
47. Bentham, *Fragment of Government,* p. 160.
48. Ibid., p. 161.
49. Ibid., pp. 215-16.
50. Ibid., p. 216.
51. Ibid., p. 236.
52. James Mill, *Essays* (London: J. Innes, n.d.), p. 32.
53. T. H. Green, *Lectures on the Principles of Political Obligation* (Ann Arbor: University of Michigan Press, 1967), p. 31.
54. Ibid., pp. 32–33.
55. Harold Laski, *Liberty in the Modern State* (New York: Harper and Row, 1930), p. 18.
56. Harold Laski, *A Grammar of Politics* (New Haven: Yale University Press, 1925), p. 24.
57. Sir Ernest Barker, *Principles of Political and Social Theory* (Oxford: Oxford University Press, 1951), p. 123.

Chapter 2

1. John Locke, *Two Treatises on Government,* 2:240. Locke raises this question no less than thirteen times—2:13, 19, 20, 89, 93, 123, 131, 136, 168, 181, 241.
2. Ibid.
3. Ibid.
4. Ibid., 2:137.
5. Ibid., 2:208.
6. There are a number of very competent assessments of recent ethical theory. See Mary Warnock, *Ethics since 1900* (New York: Oxford University Press, 1966); Carl Wellman, *The*

Language of Ethics (Cambridge: Harvard University Press, 1961); Luther J. Binkley, *Contemporary Ethical Theories* (New York: Citadel Press, 1961); Richard Brandt, *Ethical Theory* (Englewood Cliffs, N.J.: Prentice-Hall, 1959); William Frankena, *Ethics* (Englewood Cliffs, N.J.: Prentice-Hall, 1963), and "Recent Conceptions of Morality," in *Morality and the Language of Conduct*, ed. Hector-Neri Castaneda and George Nakhnikian (Detroit: Wayne State University Press, 1965), pp. 1–24. I have found the latter piece by Frankena particularly valuable.

7. R. M. Hare, *The Language of Morals* (New York: Oxford University Press, 1952), p. 69.

8. P. H. Nowell-Smith, *Ethics* (Baltimore: Penguin Books, 1954), p. 69.

9. T. M. Reed, "The Implications of Prescriptivism," *Philosophical Quarterly* 19 (October 1969), 348-51, contends that not only is Hare unable to criticize the fanatic but must even accept the fanatic's views.

10. H. L. A. Hart, *The Concept of Law* (London: Oxford University Press, 1961), pp. 53–56.

11. Kurt Baier has criticized Hart for advancing a "sophisticated attitudinal (emotive) theory" ("Moral Obligation," *American Philosophical Quarterly* 3, July 1966, p. 217), yet he is only looking at the receiving end of the "rules of recognition." The rules themselves are explained in terms of a functional or utilitarian theory. Frederick Siegler's critique is more on target, although his emphasis is on a different problem ("Hart on Rules of Obligation," *Australasian Journal of Philosophy* 45, December 1967, 341-55).

12. Stephen Toulmin, *The Place of Reason in Ethics* (London: Cambridge University Press, 1950), p. 5.

13. Ibid., p. 158.

14. Allan Gewirth, "Categorical Consistency in Ethics," *Philosophical Quarterly* 17 (October 1961), 289.

15. I should mention that this is a position greatly emphasized by existentialist ethics. Their error, however, is nearly the opposite of the theories we have been discussing. See Jean Paul Sartre, *Existentialism and Humanism* (New York: Philosophical Library, 1947).

16. The intuitionists are perhaps most guilty of forcing moral judgments into statements of reliance on another's judgment,

particularly in cases of conflicting dutes. See especially W. O. Ross, *Foundations of Ethics* (London: Oxford University Press, 1939), pp. 161–65, 321.

17. See, for instance, Henry Aiken on conscience: "It is not so much the individual conscience that determines the application of ethical norms, as it is the standard application of the terms which determines the conscience of the individual" ("Moral Philosophy and Education," *Harvard Educational Review* 25, 1955, 52). This view has been widely accepted in political science (see Karl Deutsch, *Politics and Government: How People Decide Their Fate,* Boston: Houghton Mifflin, 1970, p. 209) and has even been advanced by the pluralist revisionists (see Michael Walzer, *Obligations,* Cambridge: Harvard University Press, 1970, pp. 120–45).

18. The clearest statement of this position in traditional political thought can be found in Hobbes's *Leviathan,* ed. C. B. MacPherson (Baltimore: Penguin, 1968), pt. 2, ch. 29. See also Burke Marshall, "The Protest Movement and the Law," *University of Virginia Law Review* 51 (1965), 785; Peter Fuss, "Conscience," *Ethics* 74 (January 1969), 111–18; Final Report of the National Commission on the Causes and Prevention of Violence, *To Establish Justice, To Insure Domestic Tranquility* (Washington, D.C.: Government Printing Office, 1969), pp. 98–99; Hannah Arendt, "Civil Disobedience," *New Yorker* (September 12, 1970), pp. 70–78.

19. See H. B. Acton, "Political Action," in *Civil Disobedience: Theory and Practice,* ed. Hugo Bedau (New York: Pegasus, 1969), pp. 227–36; M. R. MacGuigan, "Civil Disobedience and Natural," *Catholic Lawyer* 11 (1965), 125; and Henry Sidgwick, *The Methods of Ethics* (Chicago: University of Chicago Press, 1962), pp. 100ff., who includes the doctrine of conscience as part of his attack on intuitionism.

20. "The 'New Radical': An Exchange," *New Politics* 4 (Fall 1965), 13, 15. The "new radicals" have now, of course, left this framework for a Marxist one. Hardly much of an advance on our terms.

21. Many students of conscience see this as a genuine dilemma and have sought resolutions. A. Campbell Garnett, "Conscience and Conscientiousness," in *Moral Concepts,* ed. Joel Feinberg (London: Oxford University Press, 1970); pp. 80–92, distin-

guishes "critical" and "uncritical" elements in conscience; Erich Fromm, *Man for Himself* (New York: Harcourt, Brace and World, 1947), pp. 92-107, separates "authoritarian" from "humanitarian" conscience; Michael Walzer, *Obligations*, attempts to guard against self-righteousness by limiting conscientious objection to an appeal to group mores. The reductio ad adsurdum, however, can be found in C. D. Broad, "Ought We to Fight for Our Country in the Next War?", in *Ethics and the History of Philosophy* (London: Routledge and Kegan Paul, 1952), pp. 232–43, who contends that since there is a coward in us all, conscientious objectors should welcome the death penalty for refusing military service as a final and convincing proof of their moral purity.

22. H. D. Lewis, "Obedience to Conscience," *Mind* 54 (July 1945), 244.

23. Ibid., pp. 244–46.

24. I must confess that it is unlikely Lewis intends his argument to be used in this manner.

25. Lewis, "Obedience to Conscience," p. 247.

26. Nowell-Smith, *Ethics*, p. 263.

27. Ibid., pp. 260–69. J. F. M. Hunter confronts the same problem when he examines the "conscience story" ("Conscience," *Mind* 72 [1963], 309–34). Both writers, however, see a solution in either/or terms.

28. This view has not, of course, been universally discarded. See Francine Gray, who reports of a Catholic priest's appeal to conscience as "the contact point between an individual and God" ("The Ultra-Resistance," *New York Review of Books* 13, September 25, 1969, 14.) See also Gunther Kuchenhoff, "Law and Conscience," *Natural Law Forum* 5 (1969), 120–31.

29. Gilbert Ryle makes this point in "Conscience and Moral Convictions," *Analysis* 7 (1940), 31–39.

30. *Hearings before the Committee on Armed Services*, U.S. Senate, 90th Congress, First Session on S. 1432, (Washington, D.C.: Government Printing Office, 1967), p. 257.

31. A few activists do indeed subscribe to this rigorous approach. See the testimony of Rev. William Sloane Coffin, Jr., in Jessica Mitford, *The Trial of Dr. Spock* (New York: Alfred A. Knopf, 1969), pp. 141–44.

32. *In Pursuit of Equity: Who Serves When Not All Serve?*,

Report of the National Advisory Commission on Selective Service (Washington, D.C.: Government Printing Office, 1967).

33. U.S. v. Seeger, 38 U.S. 163 (1965). The Court removed the religious requirement entirely in its July 15, 1970, decision in the Walker case. Objection to all wars remains a requirement of conscientious objector status.

Chapter 3

1. Robert Dahl, *Pluralist Democracy in the United States: Conflict and Consent* (Chicago: Rand McNally, 1967), p. 15.

2. Hanna Pitkin, "Obligation and Consent — I and II," *American Political Science Review* 60 (December 1965), 990–99; 61 (March 1966), 39–52. The doctrine of "hypothetical consent" is also held by C. W. Cassinelli, although his interpretation is closer to the weak version of this form of consent theory and not terribly unlike Locke's notion of tacit consent mentioned below ("The Consent of the Governed," *Western Political Quarterly* 12, 1959, 391–409).

3. Pitkin, "Obligation and Consent — II," pp. 39–40.

4. Ibid., p. 40.

5. Locke, *Two Treatises on Government,* vol. 2, par. 50, pp. 343-44; see also par. 47, p. 343. Yet when he deals with the origin of government Locke rejects the argument that historical acquiescence provides the basis for normative theory (par. 103, pp. 379–80).

6. Ibid., par. 46, p. 342

7. Ibid., par. 24, p. 326; vol. 1, par. 43, p. 206.

8. Ibid., vol. 2, par. 119, p. 392.

9. Ibid.

10. Ibid.

11. John Plamenatz, *Consent, Freedom, and Political Obligation,* rev. ed. (London: Oxford University Press, 1968), p. 24.

12. This error is also committed by Rousseau (*Social Contract and Discourses,* ed. G. D. H. Cole, New York: E. P. Dutton, 1950, p. 33). Of the traditional contract theorists only Hobbes appears to have avoided this position by contending that when one has not consented he nevertheless owes obedience out of gratitude for benefits received (*Leviathan,* pt. 1, ch. 15, p. 209).

On this point see Howard Warrender, *The Political Philosophy of Thomas Hobbes* (London: Oxford University Press, 1957), pp. 50–51.

13. H. B. Mayo, *An Introduction to Democratic Theory* (New York: Oxford University Press, 1960), p. 29; Yves Simon, *Philosophy of Democratic Government* (Chicago: University of Chicago Press, 1951); A. D. Lindsay, *The Modern Democratic State* (New York: Oxford University Press, 1962), 1:206; Leslie Lipson, *The Great Issues of Politics,* 2nd ed. (Englewood Cliffs, N.J.: Prentice-Hall, 1960), pp. 76–78, 84–85; J. R. Lucas, *The Principles of Politics* (London: Oxford University Press, 1966), pp. 284–87; Charles Frankel, *The Democratic Prospect* (New York: Harper and Row, 1962), pp. 12–13, 24–29 (Frankel does, however, offer consent as consultation or influence at pp. 33–35); R. M. Hare, "The Lawful Government," in *Philosophy, Politics, and Society,* 3rd ser., ed. Peter Laslett and W. G. Runciman (London: Basil Blackwell, 1967), pp. 157–72; Walzer, *Obligations,* pp. ix–xvi. (Walzer softens his position by extending the doctrine of consent to groups and by speaking of "diminished" obligations.)

14. Joseph Tussman, *Obligation and the Body Politic* (New York: Oxford University Press, 1966).

15. Ibid., pp. 3–7.

16. Ibid., p. 29.

17. Ibid.

18. Ibid., p. 26. A recent analysis of unanimous decision-making indicates that Tussman's position is by no means self-evident (Heinz Eulau, "Logic of Rationality in Unanimous Decision-Making," *Nomos VII: Rational Decision,* ed. Carl Friedrich, New York: Atherton, 1967, pp. 26–54).

19. Ibid., p. 27.

20. This point is ably presented by Stanley Benn and Richard Peters in *Principles of Political Thought* (New York: Free Press, 1959), p. 355.

21. Tussman, *Obligation and the Body Politic,* p. 32.

22. Ibid., p. 35.

23. Ibid., p. 36.

24. Ibid., pp. 36–37.

25. Ibid.

196 *The Shotgun behind the Door*

26. Locke, *Two Treatises,* vol. 2, par. 4, p. 309.
27. Ibid., par. 95, pp. 374–75.
28. Ibid., par. 117, p. 39.
29. Ibid., par. 121, p. 393.
30. Ibid., par. 122, p. 394.
31. Plamenatz, *Consent, Freedom, and Political Obligation,* pp 9–10.
32. Ibid., p. 23.
33. For other recent statements of this position see John J. Jenkins, "Political Consent," *Philosophical Quarterly* 18 (1968), 60–66, and D. D. Raphael, *Problems in Political Philosophy* (New York: Praeger, 1971), pp. 94–99.
34. Plamenatz, *Consent, Freedom, and Political Obligation,* p. 170. Desire and consent are reunited in Plamenatz's postscript.
35. John Plamenatz, *Man and Society,* 2 vols. (London: Longmans, 1966), 1:239–41.
36. Plamenatz, *Consent, Freedom, and Political Obligation,* pp. 170–71.
37. Hobbes, *Leviathan,* ch. 14.
38. It should be noted that I am using "agent" in its most general sense as "one who acts." This definition is not to be confused with a more specific, and perhaps more common, meaning of agent as "one who acts or does business for another."
39. Michael Walzer epitomizes what is surely a serious categorical error in democratic theory when he says, "The paradigm form of consent theory is simply, I have committed myself (consented): I am committed (obligated)" (*Obligations,* p. x).
40. Christian Bay, "Politics and Pseudo Politics: A Critical Evaluation of Some Behavioral Literature," *American Political Science Review* 59 (March 1965), 39–51.
41. Jean Piaget, *The Moral Judgment of the Child* (London: Routledge and Kegan Paul, 1932).

Chapter 4

1. *Dialogues of Plato,* ed. J. D. Kaplan, trans. Benjamin Jowett (New York: Washington Square Press, 1951), p. 54.
2. Ibid., p. 60.

3. Ibid.

4. Ibid., p. 58.

5. Ibid., p. 56. See also "Has a philosopher like you failed to discover that our country is to be more valued and higher and holier far than mother or father or any ancestor?"; ibid., p. 57.

6. Ibid., pp. 57–58.

7. Ibid., p. 57.

8. Ibid.

9. Hobbes, *Leviathan,* pt. 1, ch. 15, p. 202.

10. Ibid., p. 209. Gifts are explicitly distinguished from contracts (ch. 14, p. 193).

11. Ibid.

12. Ibid., p. 201.

13. Ibid., p. 204.

14. The moral status of gratitude is clearly higher in the *Leviathan* than in *De Cive*. In the latter Hobbes wrote that the third precept of natural law is "not a breach of trust or contract . . . therefore it is not usually termed an injury; but because good turns and thanks have a mutual eye to each other, it is called ingratitude" (*De Cive,* ed. Sterling P. Lamprecht, New York: Appleton-Century Crofts, 1949, ch. 3, p. 48). David P. Gautier argues that there is no obligation to display gratitude in Hobbes, taking in support of his position the language in *De Cive* (*The Logic of Leviathan: The Moral and Political Theory of Thomas Hobbes,* Oxford: Oxford University Press, 1969, pp. 56–57). Howard Warrender takes the position outlined in this paper but praises Hobbes's use of gratitude as a logically sound alternative to tacit consent (*The Political Philosophy of Thomas Hobbes,* Oxford: Oxford University Press, 1957, pp. 51–52). Yet, as we argue below, the soundness of the employment of gratitude is marred by Hobbes's insistence on its limited use.

15. Hobbes, *Leviathan,* pt. 2, ch. 20, p. 252; also p. 256.

16. Ibid., p. 254.

17. Ibid.

18. Ibid., p. 256.

19. Ibid., pt. 1, ch. 14, p. 193.

20. Ibid., ch. 20, p. 256.

21. Ibid.

22. Ibid., p. 255.

198   *The Shotgun behind the Door*

23. Locke, *Two Treatises of Government,* vol. 1, par. 126, p. 272.
24. Ibid., vol. 2, par. 77, p. 362; also vol. 2, par. 1, p. 38.
25. Ibid., par. 60, p. 350; par. 63, p. 352.
26. Ibid., par. 65, p 352.
27. Ibid.
28. Ibid., par. 66, p. 354; see also par. 70, pp. 356–57.
29. Ibid., par. 73, p. 358.
30. Ibid., par. 63, p. 352.
31. Ibid., par. 59, p. 349.
32. Ibid., par. 74, p. 360.
33. Ibid., par. 107, pp. 382–83.
34. Ibid., par. 121, p. 394; par. 122, p. 394.
35. The penchant for offering lists of moral duties is stronger among deontological moral philosophers. See, for instance, Sir David Ross, *The Right and the Good* (Oxford: Oxford University Press, 1930), p. 21; H. J. McCloskey, *Meta-Ethics and Normative Ethics* (The Hague: Martinus Nijhoff, 1969), pp. 222–40; John Rawls, *A Theory of Justice* (Cambridge: Harvard University Press, 1971), pp. 114–17. But even Bentham gives us a listing, although, of course, these duties are derivative in that they are tied to a felicific calculus (*The Principles of Morals and Legislation,* ed. Laurence J. Laplean, New York: Harper, 1948, pp. 121ff.).
36. J. O. Urmson has done much to introduce the concept to contemporary moral philosophers. See his "Saints and Heroes" in *Essays in Moral Philosophy,* ed. A. I. Melden (Seattle: University of Washington Press, 1958), pp. 198–216. The concept, of course, is an old one and has always been prominent in Catholic theology. See Thomas Aquinas, *Summa Theologica* (London: Bums, Oates and Washbourne, 1920), pt. 2, first pt., qu. 108, art. 4, and qu. 184, art. 3.
37. Joel Feinberg has challenged the moral accountant tendency of moral philosophers who overlook the "aging roué" who must perform "one last tremendous oversubscription" or else finish in the red. Thus what is supererogatory for the heroic doctor is mandatory for the aged sinner ("Supererogation and Rules," *Ethics* 71 [1961], 276–88). On this point more generally see Alaisdair MacIntyre, "What Morality Is Not," *Philosophy* 32 (1957), 325–35. The questions raised by both Feinberg and

MacIntyre are, of course, pertinent and can serve as a healthy goad to an accountant conception of morality. But pushed to their conclusion they represent little more than the standard intuitionist critique of the relationship between rules and ethics. Faced with the situation of a drowning man, the moral point of view is blind at least momentarily to the moral wealth of a potential rescuer. The goddess of ethics, should there be one, could care less if the rescuer were an aging roué or heroic doctor.

38. Daniel Lyons, "The Odd Debt of Gratitude," *Analysis* 29 (January 1969), 92.

39. Ibid., pp. 93–94.

40. It has, of course, been argued that the existence of the family presents more desirable patterns of special relations and therefore ought to be ended. This position usually entails a proposition that all men ought to regard each other as occupying a "special relationship" toward one another. But, if it is true that "special relationships" are the result of intimate shared experiences over time, only a vastly reordered and a distressingly carefully orchestrated social structure could produce such results.

41. Henry David Thoreau, "Resistence to Civil Government," *Henry David Thoreau* (New York: American Book, 1934), p. 246. The reverse of Thoreau's position, however, implies that uneven or nonexistent benefits are attributable to the people themselves and responsibility cannot be totally laid upon the state.

42. Although it will not be argued here, the state may owe a debt of gratitude to a soldier who participated in a war clearly unrelated to the security of the political system he represented. This, of course, involves an assumption that the war in question involved some minimal, rather than essential, security objectives and that such excursions are not prima facie immoral.

43. The tendency is for states to encourage recognition for extraordinary public service on the part of those whose work contributes to political quiescence. Those who dedicate their lives to public betterment as civil insurgents or reformers ought, by this standard, to be recognized as well.

44. This argument fits neatly with the Burkean concept of the social contract as a partnership among "those who are living, those who are dead, and those who are to be born" (*Reflections on the French Revolution,* Garden City, N.Y.: Doubleday, 1961,

p. 100). But the liberal position has generally been steadfast in its refusal to accept this version of the contract. Paine and Bentham, two very different liberals, are representative: "Those who have quitted the world and those who are not yet arrived in it are as remote from each other as the utmost stretch of the imagination can conceive. What possible obligation, then can exist between them?" ("Rights of Man," in *The Complete Writings of Thomas Paine,* 1:252); "Can it be conceived that there are men so absurd as to love posterity better than the present generation; to prefer the man who is not, to him who is; to torment the living, under pretence of promoting the happiness of those who are not born, and who may never be born?" ("Fragment on Government," in *Works of Jeremy Bentham,* 1:321). Liberal policy makers, however, have not been so scrupulous. See the inaugural addresses of Presidents Kennedy, Johnson, and Nixon.

45. John C. Livingston and Robert G. Thompson, *The Consent of the Governed* (New York: Macmillan, 1966), ch. 4.

46. *The Writings and Speeches of Edmund Burke,* 12 vols. (London: Bickers and Son, n.d.), 11:422–23.

47. "Address before the Young Men's Lyceum of Springfield, Illinois," *The Writings of Abraham Lincoln,* ed. Arthur Brooks Lapsley (New York: G. P. Putnam's Sons, 1905), 1:154–55.

48. *Public Papers of the Presidents of the U.S.: Lydon B. Johnson* (Washington, D.C.: Government Printing Office, 1967), bk. 2, p. 935.

49. Louis Hartz, *The Liberal Tradition in America* (New York: Harcourt, Brace and World, 1955), p. 302.

50. Gabriel Marcel has probably done most to present an account of gratitude independent of contractarian thought. But while his concept of "diffuse gratitude" goes far toward establishing a moral connection between the individual and the civilization of which he is a part, it is not clear that Marcel wishes that it be conceived as an account of political obligation. See "The Notion of Spiritual Heritage," in his *The Decline of Wisdom* (London: Harvie Press, 1959); *The Mystery of Being,* 2 vols. (Chicago: Henry Regnery, 1950), 1:18–38; *Man against Mass Society* (Chicago: Henry Regnery, 1952).

Chapter 5

1. H. A. Prichard, *Moral Obligation* (Oxford: Oxford University Press, 1949), p. 54.

2. Ibid., p. 55.

3. Ibid., p. 86.

4. Ibid.

5. Ibid.

6. Ibid.

7. See also E. F. Carritt, *Morals and Politics* (Oxford: Oxford University Press, 1935), who chides those who would draw a class of "political duties."

8. Compare, for instance, A. J. Ayer, *Language, Truth, and Logic* (New York: Dover, 1952), ch. 6; Ludwig Wittgenstein, Friedrich Waismann, and Rush Rhees, "Wittgenstein's Lecture on Ethics," *Philosophical Review* 74 (January 1965); C. L. Stevenson, *Ethics and Language* (New Haven: Yale University Press, 1944); William K. Frankena, "On Saying the Ethical Thing," in *Philosophy Today, No. 1*, ed. Jerry H. Gill (New York: Macmillan, 1968), pp. 250–68; J. O. Urmson, "On Grading," *Mind*.

9. For an exception see R. M. Hare, "The Lawful Government," in *Philosophy, Politics, and Society*.

10. Reprinted as "The Language of Political Theory," in *Logic and Language*, ed. A. G. Flew, 1st and 2nd ser. (Garden City, N.Y.: Doubleday, 1965).

11. Ibid., p. 191.

12. *Political Obligation* (New York: Humanities Press, 1967).

13. Ibid., p. 75.

14. Ibid., p. 85.

15. Ibid., p. 81.

16. Robert Paul Wolff, *In Defense of Anarchism* (New York: Harper and Row, 1970), pp. 13–14.

17. Ibid., p. 19.

18. Ibid., pp. 10 (n. 3), 11.

19. This position is labeled a "performative" account of political obligation below.

20. It should be mentioned that much of contemporary consent theory has attempted to avoid the problem of an *actus con-*

tractarius by deriving its structure from game theory as broadly conceived. By focusing upon existing or posited exchanges, it is thought that one can determine constitutive rules, role expectations, and even rational strategies in a political system. However, when a question is raised about the desirability of a particular constitutive rule (such as a balk in baseball or voting in politics), one is led unavoidably to a justification external to the game itself. Thus Rawls, while he insists upon the hypothetical basis of the contract as a means to construct a theory of justice, does justify one's obligation to the law as a consequence of "our having *accepted* and our *intention to continue accepting* the benefits of a just scheme of cooperation" (emphasis mine) ("Legal Obligation and the Duty of Fair Play" in *Law and Philosophy,* ed. Sidney Hook, New York: New York University Press, 1969). In his *A Theory of Justice,* Rawls moves even further away from a contractarian framework (*A Theory of Justice,* Cambridge: Harvard University Press, 1971, pp. 333–91).

21. This is fundamentally the same error that G. E. Moore fell into in his critique of naturalism. My position in regard to political obligation is the same as George Nakhnikian's, who, in response to Moore, asks for an "open question technique": the question "Is pleasure good? . . . can only work one at a time. It cannot prove that 'good' is in principle inexplicable in naturalistic terms" ("On the Naturalistic Fallacy," in *Morality and the Language of Conduct,* ed. H. Castaneda and G. Nakhnikian, pp. 145–58.)

22. Locke, *Two Treatises on Government,* vol. 2, par. 171, p .428. Unfortunately, for reasons of space it is not possible here to provide a connection between Locke's treatment of trust and his reputation as a consent theorist. The reader may wish to refer to John Dunn, "Consent in the Political Theory of John Locke," *Historical Journal* 10 (1967) 153–82, with which I agree in part and, to Gordon Schochet, ed., *Life, Liberty and Property: Essays on Locke's Political Ideas* (Belmont, Calif.: Wadsworth, 1971), pp. 6–11.

23. Locke, *Two Treatises on Government,* vols. 2, par. 201, p. 488.

24. Ibid., par. 242, p. 477.

25. Ibid., par. 137, p. 406.

26. Ibid., par. 165, p. 424.

27. For Austin's earliest formulation, see his "Other Minds," in *Philosophical Papers*, ed. J. O. Winson and G. J. Warnock (Oxford: The Clarendon Press, 1961).

28. It is not at all evident, of course, that this question is indeed tautological, since it rails to recognize a distinction among kinds of oughts. If one admits such a distinction (say, between moral and nonmoral oughts), then the question "Why ought I be moral?" is a nontautological (and important), although not necessarily answerable question. Needless to say, many moral philosophers are unwilling to accept this distinction. For representative positions see James Mish'alani, "Duty, Obligation, and Ought," *Analysis* 25 (December 1969), 33–40; Henry David Aiken, *Reason and Conduct: New Bearings in Moral Philosophy* (New York: Alfred A. Knopf, 1962), pp. 65–87; W. D. Falk, "Morality and Self and Others," in *Morality and the Language of Conduct*, pp. 25–68; Kurt Baier, "Moral Obligation," *American Philosophical Quarterly* 3 (July 1966), 211–26.

29. J. L. Austin, *How To Do Things with Words*, ed. J. O. Urmson (New York: Oxford University Press, 1962), p. 14.

30. In the course of his lectures Austin becomes a bit bolder. Performatives are successful/unsuccessful, right/wrong, correct/incorrect (ibid., pp. 115, 140). Austin concludes his essays by questioning the true/false distinction itself. "[They] do not stand for anything simple at all; but only for a general dimension of being a right or proper thing to say as opposed to a wrong thing, in these circumstances, to this audience, for these intentions" (ibid., p. 144).

31. The distinction between intention and performative in promising has been questioned by some writers. See Paul S. Ardal, "And That's a Promise," *Philosophical Quarterly* 18 (July 1968), 225–37; K. Grant, "Promises," *Mind* vol. 57 (1949); A. I. Melden, "Promising," *Mind* 65 (1956), 49–66.

32. See Tussman, *Obligation and the Body Politic;* Allen Gewirth, "Political Justice," in *Social Justice*, ed. Richard B. Brandt (Englewood Cliffs, N.J.: Prentice-Hall, 1962), pp. 128ff.; Cassinelli, "The Consent of the Governed"; Pitkin, "Obligation and Consent — I and II"; Plamenatz, *Man and Society,* 1:238–41; Walzer, *Obligations*, pp. ix–xiii.

33. Austin, *How To Do Things with Words*, pp. 147–50.

34. Ibid., pp. 150–63.

35. Of course, even these attempts at guaranteeing performance rest upon a broad trust in the functioning of social structures. A deed to a house or a will need not in themselves insure ownership or inheritance.

36. Another virtue in the consideration of political obligation in terms of trust is that it does not, at least directly, seek compliance to the state according to principles of justice, utility or public interest, terms which so frequently are defined by the state itself. It is not the injustice of a state per se which moves the citizen to renounce his allegiance to it, but that he cannot, as political authority is presently constituted, rely upon the state to be just or act in the public interest.

37. The reader is cautioned to recall the sense in which we used the word "ought" in the context of trust earlier. If an agent (citizen) says "I trust you" on the basis of rule anticipation or special characteristic reliance and does not reject trust on the basis of the subsidiary conditions, then he logically ought to frame his actions upon the stated intentions of the recipient (the state). The word "obliged" would seem to be appropriate here, but since it is so generically close to "obligation," it may fail to convey the importance of the departure involved. Therefore, I have purposely avoided it.

38. This cannot mean, however, that the state, upon the loss of its role as recipient, is free to act capriciously. The argument that one was not trusted should not be a justification for murder, lying, or stealing. In fact, the realization that one is distrusted should move one in precisely the opposite direction.

39. For an analysis of the difference between reciprocity and exploitation as well as a critique of the failure of functional analysis to consider this distinction see Alvin Gouldner, "The Norm of Reciprocity: A Preliminary Statement," *American Sociological Review* 25 (1960), 161–78.

40. H. L. A. Hart, *The Concept of Law,* is discussed below. See also the work of John Rawls, "Justice as Fairness," *Philosophical Review* 67 (1948) 164–94; "Constitutional Liberty and the Concept of Justice," *Nomos VI: Justice,* ed. Carl J. Friedrich and John W. Chapman (New York: Atherton, 1963), pp. 98–125; "The Sense of Justice," *Philosophical Review* 72 (1963), 281–305; "The Justification of Civil Disobedience," in

Civil Disobedience: Theory and Practice, ed. Hugo A. Bedau, pp. 240–55; *A Theory of Justice* (Cambridge: Harvard University Press, 1972). For criticisms of "rule-utilitarian" theories which follow the discussion below see John W. Chapman, "Justice and Fairness," in *Nomos VI: Justice,* pp. 147–69; David H. Jones, "Making and Keeping Promises," *Ethics* 76 (1965–66), 287–96; H. J. McClosky, "An Examination of Restricted Utilitarianism," *Philosophical Review* 66 (1957), 466–85.

41. The summary of Hart is from *The Concept of Law,* pp. 53–56, 83–88.

42. Wilson Carey McWilliams, "Civil Disobedience and Contemporary Constitutionalism: The American Case," *Comparative Politics* 1 (January 1968), 221–27; National Commission on the Causes and Prevention of Violence, "Civil Disobedience," in *Reflections in American Political Thought,* ed. Philip Abbott and Michael P. Riccards (New York: Intext, 1973), p. 159.

43. Thoreau, "Civil Disobedience," in *Civil Disobedience: Theory and Practice,* p. 32; M. K. Gandhi, *All Men Are Brothers* (New York: Columbia University Press, 1958), p. 148.

44. Herbert J. Storing, "The Case against Civil Disobedience," in *On Civil Disobedience: American Essays Old and New,* ed. Robert A. Goldwin (Chicago: Rand-McNally, 1970), p. 103.

45. Howard Zinn, *Disobedience and Disorder: Nine Fallacies on Law and Order* (New York: Random House, 1968), p. 103.

46. Citations from Rawls, *A Theory of Justice,* are all from sections 53–59. I have examined Rawls's work in more detail in "John Rawls and the Liberal Tradition," paper presented at the 1973 American Political Science Convention, New Orleans, Louisiana.

47. Brian Barry, *The Liberal Theory of Justice* (Oxford: Oxford University Press, 1973), p. 153.

48. Christian Bay, "Civil Disobedience: Prerequisite for Democracy in Mass Society," in *Political Theory and Social Change,* ed. David Spitz (New York: Atherton, 1967).

49. Ibid., p. 165.

50. Ibid., p. 173.

51. Ibid., pp. 173–74.

52. Ibid., p. 165.

53. Ibid., p. 168.

54. Ibid., p. 179. Bay's model here is the "piece-meal

revolutionary" who seems to be identical with the garden-variety revolutionary except that he is "less confident" that his utopia can ever be achieved.

55. Civil disobedients have become increasingly impatient with the latter restriction, tending to see constitutionalism as prima facie a weapon of the ruling class. In our account above, we have warned against constitution worship as the sole basis for trust. Perhaps it is a reaction against that interpretation that has led dissidents to this unfortunate conclusion. But a more fruitful task may involve insistence upon conditions conducive to complementation by special characteristic trust. For an able defense of this point generally see Giovonni Sartori, *Democratic Theory* (Detroit: Wayne State University Press, 1962), pp. 174–78.

Index